History 3
Student Guide

Part 2

Printed by RR Donnelley, Kendallville, IN, USA, May 2016

Table of Contents

Unit 12: Graphs, Time Lines, and Geography Review

Unit 13: The American Revolution

Answer Keys

Student Guide
Lesson 1: The Rising Ottoman Turks

- Describe the Ottoman and Mughal Empires as large and expanding Muslim empires during the Renaissance.
- Locate the Ottoman and Mughal Empires on a map.
- Describe the Ottomans as rivals for trade and territory with European countries such as Spain and Portugal.
- Recognize Hinduism and Islam as two faiths present in India.
- Identify key places and people in the Ottoman and Mughal Empires: Istanbul, Agra, the Süleymaniye mosque, the Taj Mahal, Süleyman, Akbar, and Shah Jahan.

Turkish Muslim tribes gained strength in Asia Minor, and by 1453 a weakened Constantinople fell to the rising Ottoman Turks. The victorious Turks renamed the new capital Istanbul, rebuilt the city, and laid the foundations of what would become a huge new Muslim empire.

Lesson Objectives

- Describe the Ottoman and Mughal Empires as large and expanding Muslim empires during the Renaissance.
- Locate the Ottoman and Mughal Empires on a map.
- Describe the Ottomans as rivals for trade and territory with European countries such as Spain and Portugal.
- Recognize Hinduism and Islam as two faiths present in India.
- Identify key places and people in the Ottoman and Mughal Empires: Istanbul, Agra, the Süleymaniye mosque, the Taj Mahal, Süleyman, Akbar, and Shah Jahan.
- Locate Asia Minor and the Black Sea on a map.
- Name the early Ottoman Turks as Muslim tribes from Asia Minor.
- State that the Ottoman Turks conquered Constantinople in 1453 and renamed it Istanbul.

PREPARE

Approximate lesson time is 60 minutes.

Materials

For the Student

    📖 Map of the Ottoman Empire

    History Record Book

    📖 Time Travel activity sheet

    pencils, colored 12

Keywords and Pronunciation

Amira (AH-mee-rah)

Baghdad (BAG-dad)

Istanbul (ihs-TAHN-bool)

Osman (ohs-MAHN)

Ottoman (AH-tuh-muhn)

LEARN
Activity 1: Looking Eastward *(Online)*

Activity 2: History Record Book *(Offline)*
Instructions
Choose either A or B.
A. Written Narration
Write two to four sentences explaining what the lesson was about. If necessary, use the Show You Know questions to help get started. Only include the most important parts of the lesson. Write your name, the date, and the lesson title on your written narration, and put it in your History Record Book.

Sample written narration: "The Ottoman Turks were Muslims from Asia Minor. They conquered Constantinople and named it Istanbul. Istanbul was the capital of the Ottoman Empire."

B. Picture Narration
Draw a picture of the part of the lesson that interested you most. When you have finished drawing, describe the picture. Below your picture, write a description of what you have drawn. Write your name, the date, and the lesson title on your picture narration, and put it in your History Record Book.

Activity 3: Time Travel *(Offline)*
Instructions
Enjoy your magic carpet ride one more time! Review the story in your History Reader to complete the Time Travel activity sheet.
Fill in the blanks on the time line. Mark the places on the map. Check your work with the answers below. Then use it to retell the exciting journey you took across the Arabian Peninsula and through Asia Minor.

ASSESS
Lesson Assessment: The Rising Ottoman Turks (*Online*)
You will complete an offline assessment covering the main objectives of this lesson. Your learning coach will score this assessment.

LEARN
Activity 4. Optional: The Rising Ottoman Turks *(Offline)*
Instructions

Visit your library or do some research online to learn more about the history of Istanbul. You already know two names for this interesting city, but were there more? See what you can learn about Istanbul then and now. You may want to begin with a book titled *Daily Life in Ancient and Modern Istanbul*, written by Robert Bator and illustrated by Chris Rothero (Minneapolis, MN: Lerner Publishing Group, 2000).

Name _____   ## Date _____

Time Travel

Fill in the blanks on this time line. Mark the places on the map. Then use your work to retell the story of your magic carpet ride.

600

622 The religion of Islam begins. Its founder is

_____.

800 _____ is the center of the Islamic Empire. Circle this place in red on your map.

830 The House of

_____, a place of learning, is built.

1300 The _____ Empire begins around this time. It is named for its first ruler, _____.

1453 The Ottoman Turks conquer the city of

_____. They call the city _____. Cross out the old name on the map and write in the new one.

1600

Ottoman Empire

Black Sea · Constantinople · Caspian Sea · Baghdad · Mediterranean Sea · Euphrates R. · Tigris R. · EGYPT · Nile R. · ARABIAN PENINSULA · Red Sea

N

Ottoman Empire, 1520
Ottoman Empire, 1580

0   500 miles

© 2002 K12, Inc. All rights reserved.

4

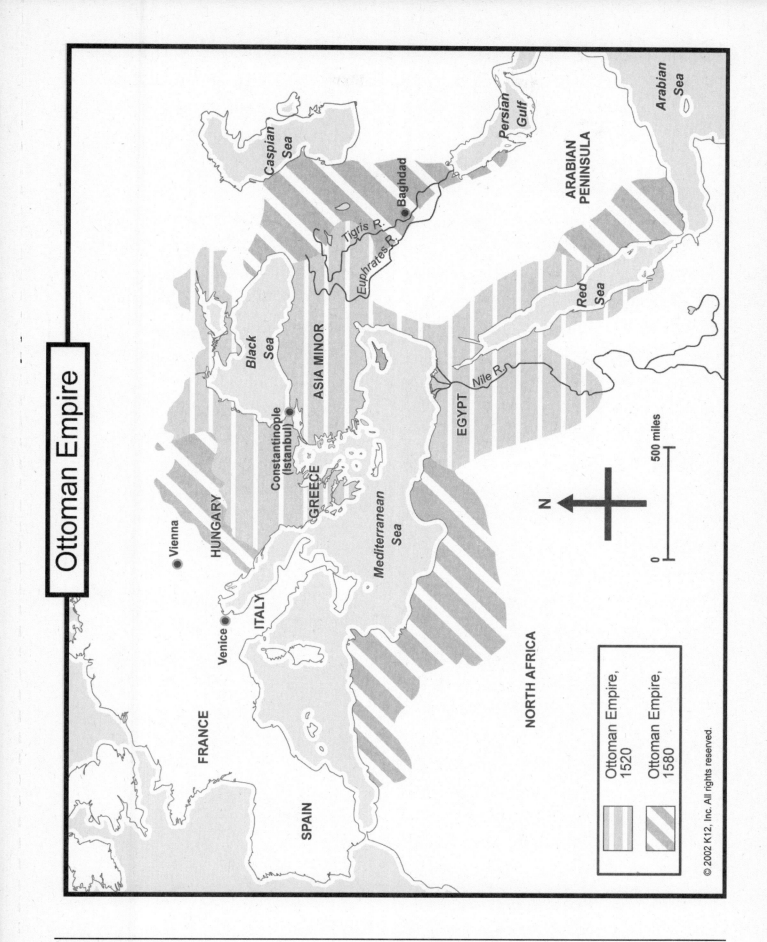

Ottoman Empire

Caspian Sea

Persian Gulf

Arabian Sea

ARABIAN PENINSULA

Baghdad

Tigris R.

Euphrates R.

Red Sea

Black Sea

ASIA MINOR

Nile R.

EGYPT

Constantinople (Istanbul)

GREECE

Mediterranean Sea

Vienna

HUNGARY

Venice

ITALY

FRANCE

NORTH AFRICA

SPAIN

N

500 miles

0

Ottoman Empire, 1520

Ottoman Empire, 1580

© 2002 K12, Inc. All rights reserved.

Lesson Assessment

The Rising Ottoman Turks

1. **In order to answer this question you will need to use the map of the Ottoman Empire.**
   Where is the Asia Minor?

2. **In order to answer this question you will need to use the map of the Ottoman Empire.**
   Where is the Black Sea?

3. What is the name of the Muslim tribes from Asia Minor we learned about today?_____

4. What city did the Ottoman Turks conquer in 1453?_____

5. What was the new name that the Ottoman Turks gave to Constantinople?_____

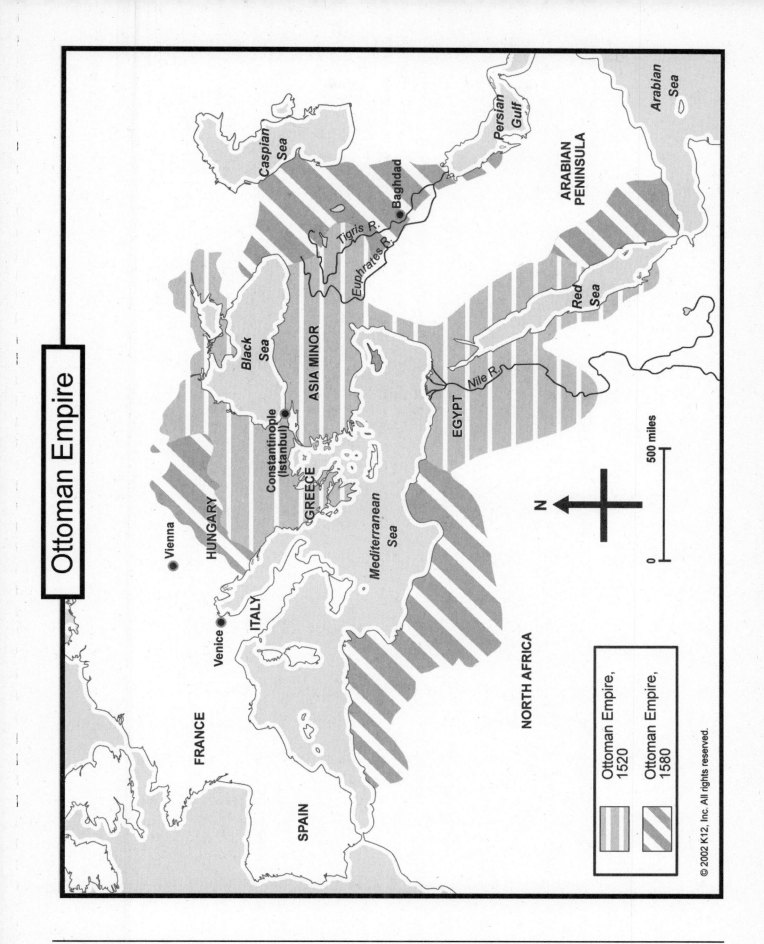

Ottoman Empire

Baghdad

Tigris R.

Euphrates R.

Caspian Sea

Persian Gulf

Arabian Sea

ARABIAN PENINSULA

Red Sea

Nile R.

EGYPT

ASIA MINOR

Black Sea

Constantinople (Istanbul)

GREECE

Vienna

HUNGARY

Mediterranean Sea

Venice

ITALY

FRANCE

SPAIN

NORTH AFRICA

N

500 miles

0

Ottoman Empire, 1520

Ottoman Empire, 1580

© 2002 K12, Inc. All rights reserved.

Student Guide
Lesson 2: Süleyman, the Lawgiver

Süleyman I led the Ottoman Empire at the height of its power and glory. Ruling for more than 40 years, he expanded the empire and gave it a single set of laws. He was known to westerners as Süleyman the Magnificent and to his subjects as Süleyman the Lawgiver.

Lesson Objectives

- Locate the Ottoman Empire on a map.
- Identify Süleyman I as an important leader of the Ottoman Empire.
- Explain that Süleyman I expanded the empire and organized its laws.

PREPARE

Approximate lesson time is 60 minutes.

Materials

For the Student

    📖 Map of the Ottoman Empire

    History Record Book

    📖 Süleyman: More than Magnificent activity sheet

    pencils, colored 12

Keywords and Pronunciation

Muhibbi (moh-HEEB-bee)

sultan : A king or ruler of a Muslim state.

Süleyman (suhlay-MAHN)

Süleymaniye (suhlay-MAHN-ee-yeh)

LEARN
Activity 1: The Many Names of Süleyman *(Online)*

Activity 2: History Record Book *(Offline)*

Instructions

Choose either A or B.

A. Written Narration

Write two to four sentences explaining what the lesson was about. If necessary, use the Show You Know questions to help get started. Only include the most important parts of the lesson. Write your name, the date, and the lesson title on your written narration, and put it in your History Record Book.

Sample written narration: "Süleyman I was the ruler of the Ottoman Empire. He helped make the empire bigger and stronger. The people called him by many names. They called him Süleyman the Lawgiver because he organized the laws."

B. Picture Narration

Draw a picture of the part of the lesson that interested you most. When you have finished drawing, describe the picture. Below your picture, write a description of what you have drawn. Write your name, the date, and the lesson title on your picture narration, and put it in your History Record Book.

Activity 3: Süleyman: More than Magnificent (Offline)
Instructions

One of the names often given to Süleyman is "the Magnificent." The story mentions many others, including "Sultan of Sultans," "Master of the World," "Caesar," "the Lawgiver," "the Just," "Muhibbi, the Loving," and "the Builder."

During his reign, Süleyman did many things that led him to be called by these names. Look at the Süleyman: More than Magnificent activity sheet, where you'll see illustrations of some of the things this remarkable ruler did.

Choose one of Süleyman's names from the word box and write it under the picture that best illustrates what it means. Then color each picture if you like.

For a challenge, illustrate one of Süleyman's other names on the back and label your picture.

ASSESS
Lesson Assessment: Süleyman, the Lawgiver (Online)

You will complete an offline assessment covering the main objectives of this lesson. Your learning coach will score this assessment.Learning

---

LEARN
Activity 4. Optional: Süleyman, the Lawgiver (Online)

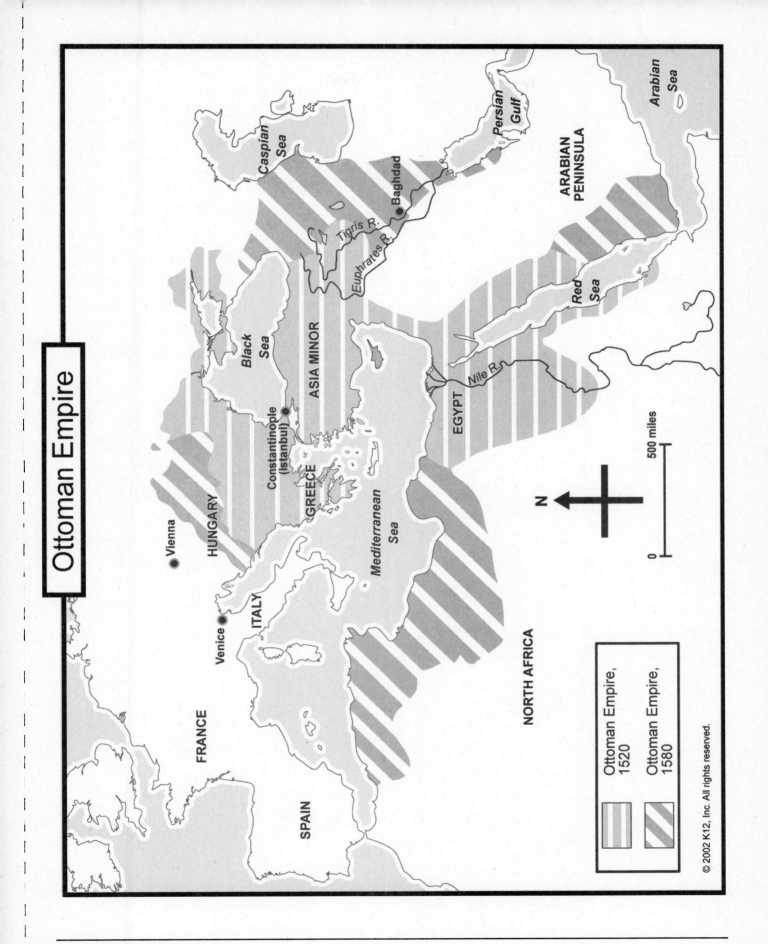

Ottoman Empire

Caspian Sea

Persian Gulf

Arabian Sea

ARABIAN PENINSULA

Baghdad

Tigris R.

Euphrates R.

Red Sea

Black Sea

ASIA MINOR

Nile R.

EGYPT

Constantinople (Istanbul)

GREECE

HUNGARY

Vienna

Mediterranean Sea

ITALY

Venice

FRANCE

SPAIN

NORTH AFRICA

N

500 miles

0

Ottoman Empire, 1520

Ottoman Empire, 1580

© 2002 K12, Inc. All rights reserved.

<u>Name</u>   <u>Date</u>

Süleyman: More than Magnificent

Choose the name in the word box that matches what you see about Süleyman in each picture. Write the name under the picture and color it. For a challenge, draw and label your own Süleyman picture on the back.

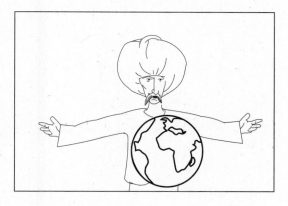

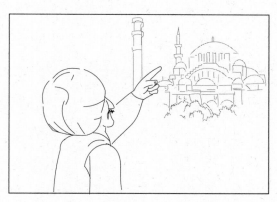

sultan of sultans	master of the world	Caesar	the lawgiver
the just	Muhibbi the loving	the builder	

Name _____   Date _____

Lesson Assessment

Süleyman, the Lawgiver

1. **In order to answer this question you will need to use the map of the Ottoman Empire.** Where is the Ottoman Empire?

2. Which sultan ruled the Ottoman Empire during its most powerful years?_____

3. Did the Ottoman Empire get larger or smaller under Süleyman?_____

4. Why did the people of Turkey remember Süleyman I as "Süleyman, the

   Lawgiver"?_____

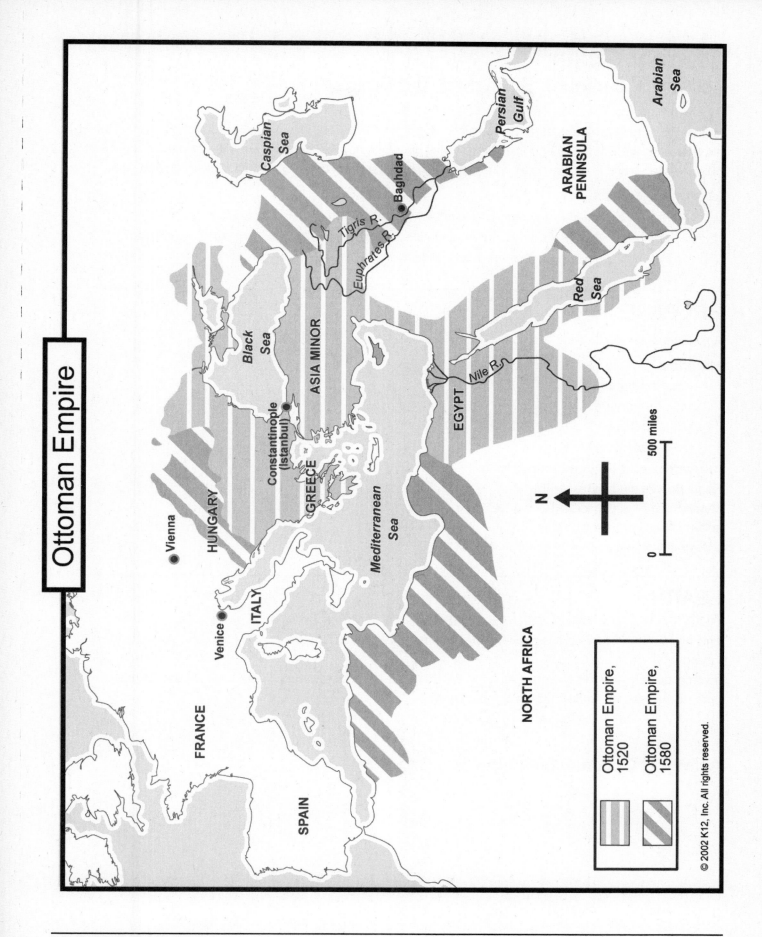

Ottoman Empire

Caspian Sea

Persian Gulf

Arabian Sea

ARABIAN PENINSULA

Baghdad

Tigris R.

Euphrates R.

Red Sea

Black Sea

ASIA MINOR

Nile R.

EGYPT

Constantinople (Istanbul)

GREECE

HUNGARY

Vienna

Mediterranean Sea

ITALY

Venice

FRANCE

NORTH AFRICA

SPAIN

N

500 miles

0

Ottoman Empire, 1520

Ottoman Empire, 1580

© 2002 K12, Inc. All rights reserved.

19

Student Guide
Lesson 3. Optional: Süleyman, the Builder

Like the leaders of the European Renaissance, Süleyman (1489-1588) loved architecture and the arts. During his reign over the Ottoman Empire, he made Istanbul one of the most beautiful and vibrant cities in the world. Süleyman left a rich legacy of amazing mosques, bridges, and public baths, as well as painting and verse.

Lesson Objectives
- Name Süleyman as a person who loved and supported art and architecture.
- Name two kinds of buildings or monuments Süleyman had built in Istanbul, such as palaces, mosques, public baths, fountains, and bridges.

PREPARE

Approximate lesson time is 60 minutes.

Materials
> For the Student
>> History Record Book
>> 🖳 Comparing Two Buildings activity sheet
>> paper, notebook

Keywords and Pronunciation
Hagia Sophia (HAH-juh soh-FEE-uh)
Mimar Koca Sinan (mee-MAHR koh-JEH see-NAHN)
sultan : A king or ruler of a Muslim state.
Süleymaniye (suhlay-MAHN-ee-yeh)

LEARN
Activity 1. Optional: Optional Lesson Instructions (Online)
This lesson is OPTIONAL. It is provided for students who seek enrichment or extra practice. You may skip this lesson.

If you choose to skip this lesson, then go to the Plan or Lesson Lists page and mark this lesson "Skipped" in order to proceed to the next lesson in the course.

Activity 2. Optional: Sinan Builds a City (Online)

Activity 3. Optional: History Record Book (Offline)
Instructions
Choose either A or B.
A. Written Narration
Write two to four sentences explaining what the lesson was about. If necessary, use the Show You Know questions to help get started. Only include the most important parts of the lesson. Write your name, the date, and the lesson title on your written narration, and put it in your History Record Book.

Sample written narration: "Süleyman wanted Istanbul to be full of beautiful art and buildings. Sinan designed many wonderful buildings for him. He built a great mosque. He built schools, hospitals, and fountains."

B. Picture Narration
Draw a picture of the part of the lesson that interested you most. When you have finished drawing, describe the picture. Below your picture, write a description of what you have drawn. Write your name, the date, and the lesson title on your picture narration, and put it in your History Record Book.

Activity 4. Optional: Comparing Two Buildings (Offline)
Instructions

Look closely at the Süleymaniye Mosque, and remember the sultan for whom it is named. Look closely, too, at the Hagia Sophia, which was also mentioned in the Reading Room story. Originally built as a Christian church, the Hagia Sophia later became a mosque, and is now a museum. The words "Hagia Sophia" mean "holy wisdom" in Greek.	Complete the diagram on the Comparing Two Buildings activity sheet. Decide how these two buildings are alike and different. Write a sentence that explains one way they are alike. Write another sentence that explains one way they are different. Write one more sentence that tells why you might want to see both buildings.
Hagia Sophia	**Süleymaniye mosque**

Activity 5. Optional: Süleyman, the Builder (Online)

Name _____   Date _____

Comparing Two Buildings

Decide which of the buildings each phrase describes and write it where it belongs in the diagram. Then use your diagram to write one sentence about how these buildings are alike, one about how they are different, and one about why people might want to visit both.

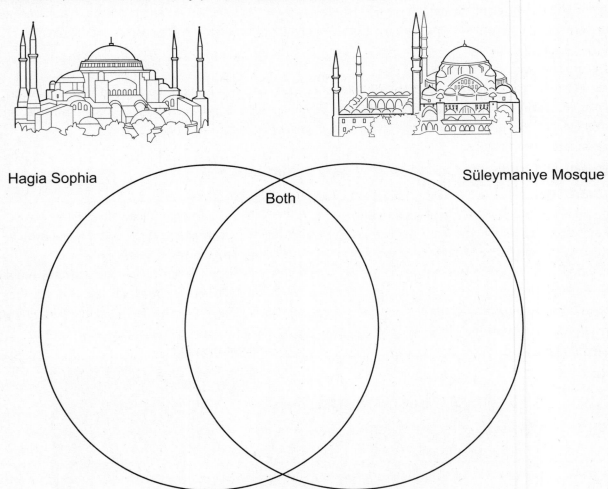

Hagia Sophia   Süleymaniye Mosque

Both

Phrases Describing the Buildings

beautiful building   tall towers (minarets) outside
built as a Muslim place of worship   built as a Christian church
named for 10th sultan   has a dome
designed and built by Sinan   built first
located in Istanbul   contains tombs
name means "holy wisdom"

Student Guide
Lesson 4: The Trading Turks

The Ottoman Turks were central to world trade, linking the Middle East, East Asia, India, Arabia, and Europe. The Grand Bazaar in Istanbul sold goods from all over the world.

Lesson Objectives
- State that the Ottoman Turks were skilled traders.
- Name some products sold at the Grand Bazaar in Istanbul.
- Name three places where the Ottoman Turks traded.
- Identify the crescent and star as symbols of Islam.

PREPARE

Approximate lesson time is 60 minutes.

Materials
For the Student
- Map of the Ottoman Empire
- globe, inflatable
- History Record Book

Optional
- crayons 8

Keywords and Pronunciation
caravan : A group of travelers on a journey, often with pack animals such as camels or mules.
Kamil (kah-MIHL)
Murad (moo-RAHT)
Nadia (NAH-dee-uh)
Tariq (tah-RIK)
trade : The exchange of goods, services, or money.

LEARN
Activity 1: Trade and the Ottoman Turks (Online)

Activity 2: History Record Book (Offline)

Instructions

Choose either A or B.

A. Written Narration

Write two to four sentences explaining what the lesson was about. If necessary, use the Show You Know questions to help get started. Only include the most important parts of the lesson. Write your name, the date, and the lesson title on your written narration, and put it in your History Record Book.

Sample written narration: "The Ottoman Turks had a great empire. They traded with many lands like India, China, and North Africa. They traded silk, spices, and other things at the Grand Bazaar."

B. Picture Narration

Draw a picture of the part of the lesson that interested you most. When you have finished drawing, describe the picture. Below your picture, write a description of what you have drawn. Write your name, the date, and the lesson title on your picture narration, and put it in your History Record Book.

Activity 3: Learning the Language of Trade (Offline)

Instructions

The word *trade* means "exchange goods, services, or money." In this lesson, you learned that the Turks were great traders.

Let's review some of the words and phrases that told about trade. See if you can remember them by reading their definitions. Write the words down on a sheet of paper as you think of them. The first letter of each word is there to give you a hint.

1. When people pay money for something, they b_____ it.
2. When people get money for something, they s_____ it.
3. All the things the Ottoman Turks traded are called g_____.
4. The large place where people came to trade things from all over the world was called the G_____ B_____.
5. A name for one of the places where Tariq traded is a m_____.
6. A metal that Tariq traded, which was sometimes made into coins and used as money, is g_____.
7. If something is available for someone else to buy, it is f_____ s_____.

Now use at least five of these words to write a message from Tariq to his family describing what he has been doing at the covered market of Istanbul.

ASSESS

Lesson Assessment: The Trading Turks (*Online*)

You will complete an offline assessment covering the main objectives of this lesson. Your learning coach will score this assessment.

LEARN

Activity 4. Optional: The Trading Turks (*Online*)

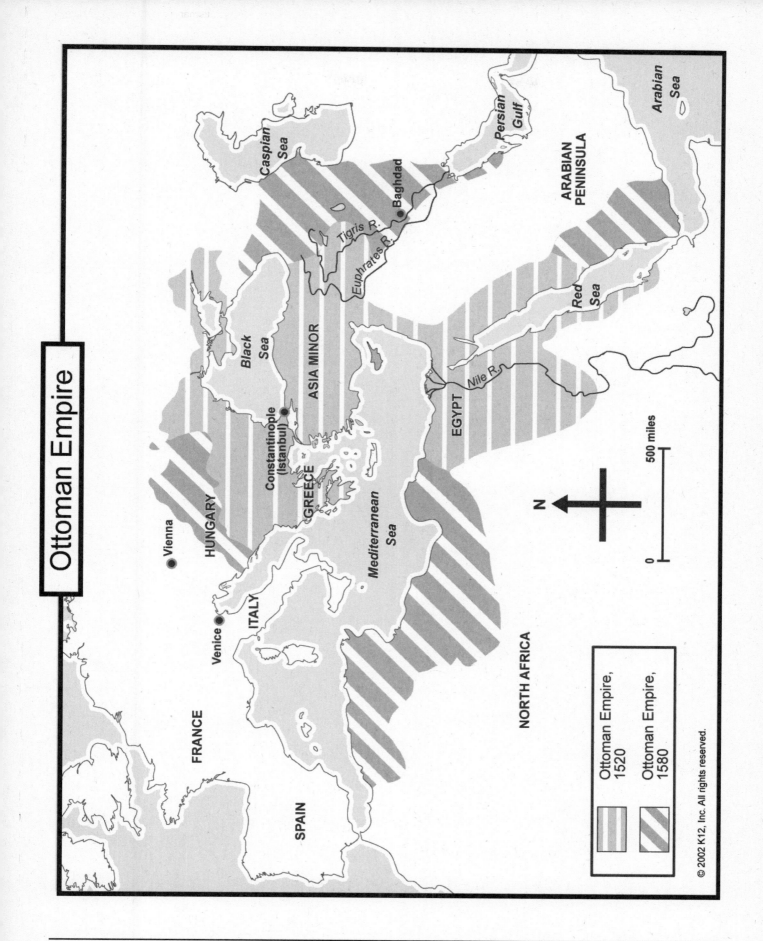

Ottoman Empire

Caspian Sea

Persian Gulf

Arabian Sea

ARABIAN PENINSULA

Baghdad

Tigris R.

Euphrates R.

Black Sea

ASIA MINOR

Red Sea

Nile R.

Constantinople (Istanbul)

EGYPT

GREECE

Vienna

HUNGARY

ITALY

Venice

Mediterranean Sea

FRANCE

NORTH AFRICA

SPAIN

N

500 miles

0

Ottoman Empire, 1520

Ottoman Empire, 1580

© 2002 K12, Inc. All rights reserved.

Lesson Assessment

The Trading Turks

1. Because of their large empire, what were the Ottoman Turks particularly good at? _____

2. What were some of the products sold at the Grand Bazaar in

    Istanbul? _____

3. Name three parts of the world where Ottoman merchants

    traded? _____

4. Think about the Turkish flag. What traditional symbols of Islam appear on it? _____

Student Guide
Lesson 5: Mughals Victorious in India

The birthplace of Hinduism, India was ruled by various Muslim dynasties from the late twelfth century on. In 1526, Muslim invaders from Afghanistan founded the Mughal Empire.

Lesson Objectives

- Locate the Indian subcontinent on a map and name the Indus and Ganges as India's two main rivers.
- Explain that many people wanted spices and gems from India.
- State that Hinduism was the main religion of India.
- Name the Mughal Empire as the powerful Muslim empire established in India.

PREPARE

Approximate lesson time is 60 minutes.

Materials

For the Student

    📖 Map of the Indian Subcontinent

    History Record Book

    📖 Hinduism and Islam activity sheet

    pencils, colored 12

Keywords and Pronunciation

Babur (BAH-bur)

Ganges (GAN-jeez)

Gangetic (gan-JEH-tik)

Himalayas (hih-muh-LAY-uhz)

Hindus (HIN-doos)

Hindustan (hin-doo-STAN)

Indus (IN-duhs)

Mughal (MOO-guhl)

subcontinent : A landmass of great size but smaller than one of the seven main continents.

LEARN
Activity 1: Babur Solves a Problem *(Online)*

Activity 2: History Record Book (Offline)

Instructions

Choose either A or B.

A. Written Narration

Write two to four sentences explaining what the lesson was about. If necessary, use the Show You Know questions to help get started. Only include the most important parts of the lesson. Write your name, the date, and the lesson title on your written narration, and put it in your History Record Book.

Sample written narration: "India is a huge subcontinent in Asia. Most of the people living there were Hindus. Babur conquered a lot of land and started the Mughal Empire in India. He built mosques beside Hindu temples."

B. Picture Narration

Draw a picture of the part of the lesson that interested you most. When you have finished drawing, describe the picture. Below your picture, write a description of what you have drawn. Write your name, the date, and the lesson title on your picture narration, and put it in your History Record Book.

Activity 3: Comparing Hinduism and Islam (Offline)

Instructions

When Babur arrived in India, he found that the people there did not follow his religion of Islam. Their religion was Hinduism, and they worshipped many gods.

Print the Hinduism and Islam activity sheet to review more about Hinduism, to see pictures of three Hindu gods, and to compare this religion with Babur's.

ASSESS

Lesson Assessment: Mughals Victorious in India (Online)

You will complete an offline assessment covering the main objectives of this lesson. Your learning coach will score this assessment.

Name _____   Date _____

Hinduism and Islam

Review the information about Hinduism and answer the questions about Islam. Then color the pictures if you wish.

Brahma

Vishnu

Shiva

Hindus believe that Brahman is the great spirit that lives in all things.
What is the name of the God that Muslims believe in?

_____

Brahma, Vishnu, and Shiva are just three of the many Hindu gods and
goddesses. How many gods are there in Islam? _____

The Hindus built temples as their places of worship. What are Muslim
places of worship called? _____

The Vedas are holy books that are a collection of Hindu hymns, prayers,
laws, and stories. What is the name of the holy book of Islam?

_____

Answers: Allah, one, mosques, Koran

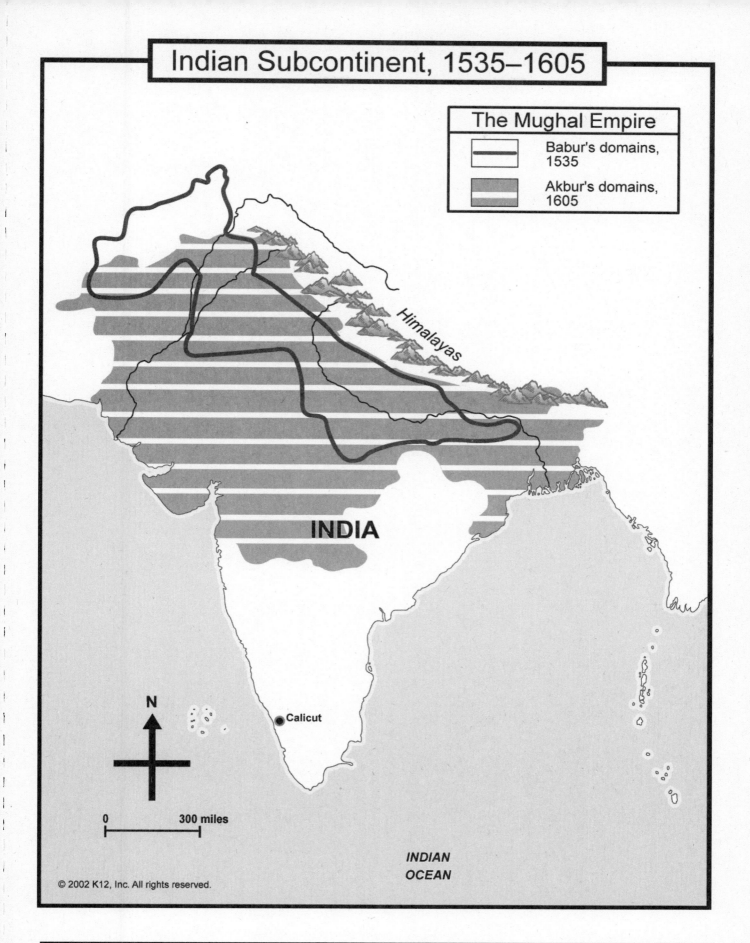

Indian Subcontinent, 1535–1605

The Mughal Empire

- Babur's domains, 1535
- Akbur's domains, 1605

Himalayas

INDIA

N

● Calicut

0   300 miles

INDIAN OCEAN

Lesson Assessment

Mughals Victorious in India

1. **In order to answer this question you will need to use the map of the Indian Subcontinent.**
   Where is the Indian Subcontinent?

2. What are India's two main rivers? _____

3. Why were Europeans and central Asians so interested in India? _____

4. What was the ancient religion followed by most people in India at this time? _____

5. What was the name of the powerful Muslim empire founded by Babur in India? _____

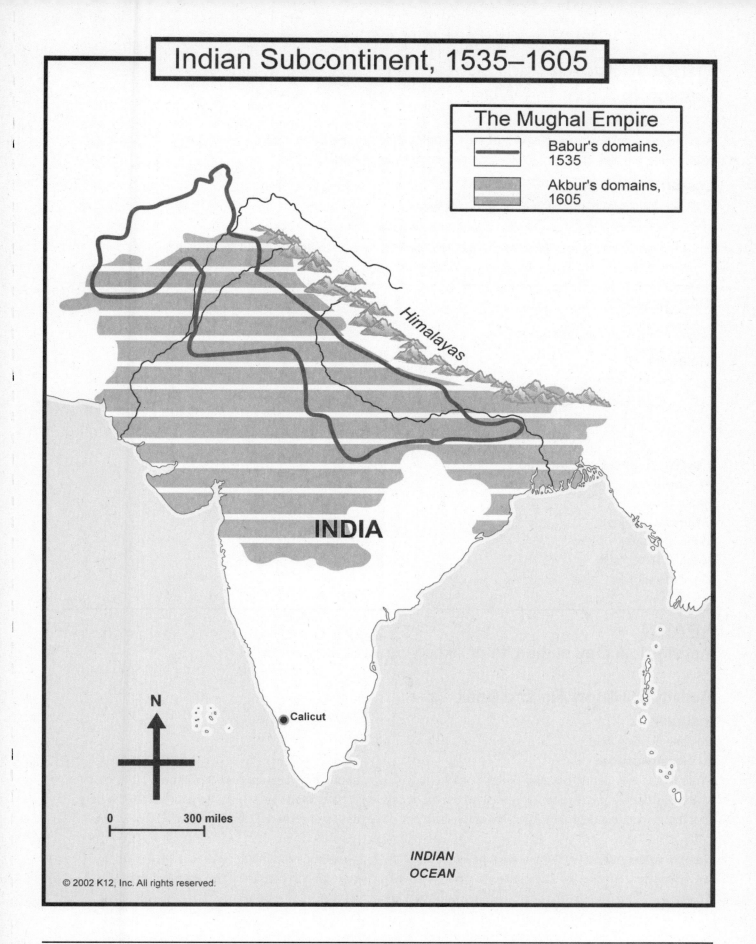

Indian Subcontinent, 1535–1605

The Mughal Empire

- Babur's domains, 1535
- Akbur's domains, 1605

Himalayas

INDIA

N

Calicut

0   300 miles

INDIAN
OCEAN

Student Guide
Lesson 6: Akbar the Wise

Akbar is considered the wisest and greatest Mughal Emperor. He ruled India for nearly half a century and established a policy of religious toleration for all the faiths of India.

Lesson Objectives
- Identify Akbar as a great Mughal emperor.
- Describe Akbar as a Muslim ruler interested in all religions.
- State that Akbar worked to make sure people of different religions could live together in peace.

PREPARE

Approximate lesson time is 60 minutes.

Materials
For the Student
- 📖 Map of the Indian Subcontinent
- History Record Book
- paper, notebook

Keywords and Pronunciation
Akbar (AK-bur)
Babur (BAH-bur)
Ganges (GAN-jeez)
Indus (IN-duhs)
Mughal (MOO-guhl)
Zia (ZEE-yah)

LEARN
Activity 1: A Day in the Life of Akbar (Online)

Activity 2: History Record Book (Offline)
Instructions
Choose either A or B.

A. Written Narration
Write two to four sentences explaining what the lesson was about. If necessary, use the Show You Know questions to help get started. Only include the most important parts of the lesson. Write your name, the date, and the lesson title on your written narration, and put it in your History Record Book.

Sample written narration: "Akbar was the emperor of the Mughal Empire in India. He was a wise ruler. There were Muslims, Hindus, and Christians living in his empire. Akbar tried to help them live together in peace."

B. Picture Narration

Draw a picture of the part of the lesson that interested you most. When you have finished drawing, describe the picture. Below your picture, write a description of what you have drawn. Write your name, the date, and the lesson title on your picture narration, and put it in your History Record Book.

Activity 3: Speaking of Akbar *(Offline)*

Instructions

Imagine that Akbar's servant Zia was attending a gathering with his friends, and they asked him to describe Akbar. What do you think Zia would say?

Suppose he began with the sentence "Akbar is a very wise man indeed." Your job is to write the rest of Zia's speech so that it supports the first sentence. Help Zia persuade his friends that Akbar was a great Mughal emperor. Write your speech. Then say it to someone else.

If you need more information and ideas, visit the Akbar - The Great website about Akbar. You'll find out more about his reign, and you'll also have a chance to read an "interview" with him.

ASSESS

Lesson Assessment: Akbar the Wise (*Offline*)

You will complete an offline assessment covering the main objectives of this lesson. Your learning coach will score this assessment.

Indian Subcontinent, 1535–1605

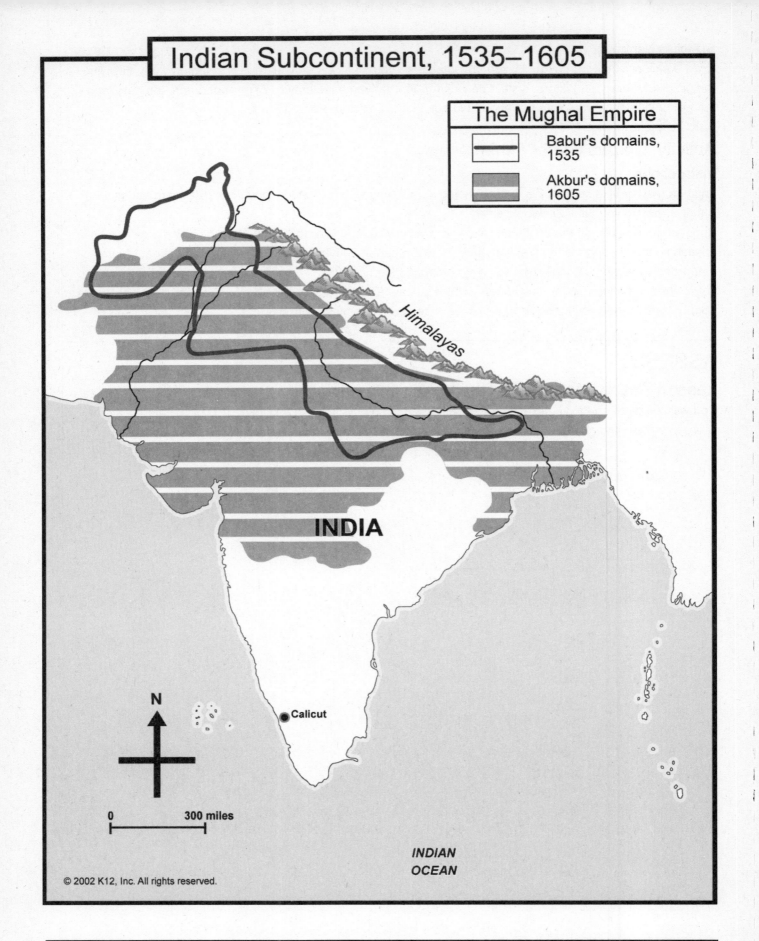

The Mughal Empire

Babur's domains, 1535

Akbur's domains, 1605

Himalayas

INDIA

Calicut

N

0   300 miles

INDIAN OCEAN

Lesson Assessment

Akbar the Wise

1. Which empire did Akbar rule so well?_____

2. What was Akbar's religion?_____

3. Was Akbar interested in just the Muslim religion?_____

4. What did Akbar work to do for people of different religions?_____

Student Guide
Lesson 7: Shah Jahan Builds the Taj Mahal

Leading the Mughal Empire during a golden age of art and architecture, Shah Jahan spent freely on splendid architecture. The Taj Mahal, a magnificent tomb for his favorite wife, is still India's most famous building.

Lesson Objectives

- Name Shah Jahan as a Mughal emperor who built the Taj Mahal.
- Describe the Taj Mahal as a beautiful tomb for Shah Jahan's wife.
- Name some characteristics of the Taj Mahal (such as its enormous dome, minarets, and use of marble).
- Identify the Taj Mahal from a set of images.

PREPARE

Approximate lesson time is 60 minutes.

Materials

For the Student

History Record Book

Taj Mahal: Magnificent Then and Now activity sheet

Keywords and Pronunciation

inlay : To set into another surface, such as stone.

minarets (min-uh-RETS)

Shah Jahan (shah juh-HAHN)

Taj Mahal (tahj mah-HAHL)

LEARN
Activity 1: A Tour of the Taj Mahal *(Online)*

Activity 2: History Record Book *(Offline)*
Instructions

Choose either A or B.

A. Written Narration

Write two to four sentences explaining what the lesson was about. If necessary, use the Show You Know questions to help get started. Only include the most important parts of the lesson. Write your name, the date, and the lesson title on your written narration, and put it in your History Record Book.

Sample written narration: "An emperor named Shah Jahan built the Taj Mahal. He built it to be a tomb for his wife. The Taj Mahal has tall domes, towers, and gardens. It's one of the most beautiful buildings in the world."

B. Picture Narration

Draw a picture of the part of the lesson that interested you most. When you have finished drawing, describe the picture. Below your picture, write a description of what you have drawn. Write your name, the date, and the lesson title on your picture narration, and put it in your History Record Book.

Activity 3: A Visit to the Taj Mahal *(Offline)*
Instructions

The Taj Mahal was Shah Jahan's magnificent tomb for his wife. During this lesson, you took a tour of this fabulous structure. Now you'll have a chance to write an article about it for your local newspaper. Review the lesson and share your observations. Be sure to include as much as you can about the history of the Taj Mahal.

ASSESS

Lesson Assessment: Shah Jahan Builds the Taj Mahal *(Online)*

You will complete an offline assessment covering the main objectives of this lesson. Your learning coach will score this assessment.

Name _____   Date _____

Taj Mahal: Magnificent Then and Now

Yesterday our lead reporter,

_____

visited the Taj Mahal in Agra, India. The report below details the visit and the history of this famous structure.

Name _____   Date _____

Lesson Assessment

Shah Jahan Builds the Taj Mahal

1. Who was the Mughal emperor who built the Taj Mahal?_____

2. Why did Shah Jahan build the Taj Mahal?_____

3. What are some of the characteristics of the Taj Mahal?_____

4. Select the Taj Mahal from the three images shown.

A.

B.

C.

Student Guide
Lesson 8: Unit Review and Assessment

You've completed this unit, and now it's time to review what you've learned and take the unit assessment.

Lesson Objectives

- Demonstrate mastery of important knowledge and skills in this unit.
- Name the early Ottoman Turks as Muslim tribes from Asia Minor.
- State that the Ottoman Turks conquered Constantinople in 1453 and renamed it Istanbul.
- Locate the Ottoman Empire on a map.
- Explain that Süleyman I expanded the empire and organized its laws.
- State that the Ottoman Turks were skilled traders.
- Identify the crescent and star as symbols of Islam.
- Locate the Indian subcontinent on a map and name the Indus and Ganges as India's two main rivers.
- State that Hinduism was the main religion of India.
- Name the Mughal Empire as the powerful Muslim empire established in India.
- State that Akbar worked to make sure people of different religions could live together in peace.
- Describe the Taj Mahal as a beautiful tomb for Shah Jahan's wife.
- Identify the Taj Mahal from a set of images.

PREPARE

Approximate lesson time is 60 minutes.

Materials

For the Student

History Record Book

Keywords and Pronunciation

Akbar (AK-bur)
Baghdad (BAG-dad)
Byzantine (BIH-zn-teen)
Istanbul (ihs-TAHN-bool)
minarets (min-uh-RETS)
Mughal (MOO-guhl)
Ottoman (AH-tuh-muhn)
Shah Jahan (shah juh-HAHN)
Süleyman (suhlay-MAHN)
Taj Mahal (tahj mah-HAHL)

LEARN
Activity 1: A Look Back (Offline)
Instructions

We've learned that the Renaissance was a time of rebirth in Europe. It was an age of exploration and discovery. Strong new monarchs rose in Spain, France, and England. In Italy powerful leaders emerged in the busy city-states. They patronized art and built beautiful new palaces. These rulers competed with each other for land and trade. They fought with each other about religion, too--about whether their nations should be Catholic or Protestant.

But European rulers knew their biggest rivals for land and trade came not from other European kingdoms, but from the east. The new monarchs in Christian Europe led kingdoms that were tiny compared to the growing new Muslim empires in the east. The two largest empires in the world during the Renaissance were the two we have just studied. What were their names? [1]

Let's play "what do we know about the Ottoman Empire?" Where did the Ottoman Empire start? Hint: It's a peninsula ringed by the Mediterranean Sea in the south and the Black Sea in the north. [2] We learned that Arab armies and traders spread Islam into Asia Minor and Central Asia during the Middle Ages. By the 1300s, one Muslim tribe in Asia Minor became very powerful. What was the name of that tribe? [3]

The Ottoman Turks gave Europeans a scare and themselves a new home when they took over Constantinople in 1453. The old capital of the Byzantine Empire became the new capital of the Ottoman Turks. Do you remember what the Turks renamed their new capital? [4] One great Ottoman leader would make Istanbul sparkle as it never had before. What's the name of that famous Ottoman ruler? [5]

Whether you called him "Süleyman, the Magnificent," "Süleyman, the Lawgiver," or "Süleyman, the Builder," he made a big difference. The Ottoman Empire grew huge during his reign. Ottoman Turks ruled lands along the Mediterranean in Europe and faraway North Africa. They ruled Baghdad in Persia, the holy cities of Arabia, and parts of Italy, too. To rule such a large empire, they needed good laws. So what did Süleyman do? [6]

Trade was brisk in the Ottoman Empire. Ottoman merchants brought silk from China, wool from Florence, and spices from India to Istanbul's Grand Bazaar. When merchants from around the world came to Istanbul, they knew they were in a great city. Süleyman built beautiful new mosques, fountains, baths, and palaces there. But the Ottomans didn't control all of the east. In fact, the spices of India came from another great Muslim empire. What was the name of the Muslim empire ruling in India? [7]

The Mughals conquered India at about the same time the Ottomans were conquering Istanbul. The Mughals were not Ottomans. But they were Muslim, and they had a special problem to solve. They had to figure out how to rule India, a land with millions of people, most of whom were not Muslim.

What was the faith of most Indians when the Mughals conquered India? [8] Early Mughal leaders decided to build Muslim mosques right next to Hindu temples. They wanted to show how powerful Islam was. But one famous Mughal leader was interested in all religions. He was interested in making sure that the people of different religions could live in peace. He even married a Hindu woman. Can you remember his name? [9]

Akbar the Wise ruled for many years. He ruled when the Portuguese arrived in India. He was even interested in those Catholic priests the Portuguese brought with them.

It was Akbar's grandson, Shah Jahan, who gave the world India's most famous building. What's the name of the tomb Shah Jahan built for his wife? [10] That beautiful marble building attracts visitors from all over the world today. Its style is Muslim--domes, minarets, inlay, and writing from the Koran. But its beauty is universal. Everyone can enjoy looking at it.

The Ottoman Empire and the Mughal Empire, the two great Muslim empires of the Renaissance, were like the Christian kingdoms of Europe in many ways. Their rulers were interested in art, building, and trade. They were passionate about religion. Just as Christian kingdoms in Europe often fought with each other, Muslims often fought other Muslims. And like the Christian kingdoms in Europe, the large Muslim empires of the Ottomans and the Mughals enjoyed a golden age in the Renaissance.

Activity 2: History Record Book Review (Offline)
Instructions
Use the contents of your History Record Book to review the unit on Looking East: Ottomans and Mughals. Take some time to revisit the narrations, activity sheets, writing activities, and pictures in the History Record Book. Read the narrations aloud. Don't hurry this part of the review; it will refresh your memory and give you a sense of just how much you've already learned.

Activity 3: Online Interactive Review (Online)

ASSESS
Unit Assessment: Looking East: Ottomans and Mughals (Offline)
Complete an offline Unit Assessment. Your learning coach will score this part of the Assessment.

Name _____   Date _____

Looking East: Ottomans and Mughals

Read each question and its answer choices. Fill in the bubble in front of the word or words that best answer the question.

Questions marked with an asterisk (*) will have more than one correct answer. For these questions, fill in the bubble next to ALL correct answers.

1. Which Muslim tribes conquered Constantinople and renamed it when they made it their capital?
   - ⓐ Indian Mughals
   - ⓑ Ottoman Turks
   - ⓒ Hindus
   - ⓓ Berbers

2. The new name for Constantinople was _____.
   - ⓐ Istanbul
   - ⓑ St. Petersburg
   - ⓒ Mecca
   - ⓓ Medina

3. What symbol of Islam do you often see on flags?
   - ⓐ cross and shield
   - ⓑ eagle and snake
   - ⓒ crescent and star
   - ⓓ dome and moon

4. When the Mughals conquered India, what religion did most of the people there practice?
- ⓐ Hinduism
- ⓑ Christianity
- ⓒ Islam
- ⓓ Judaism

5. What building did Shah Jahan build as a tomb for his wife?
- ⓐ Hagia Sophia
- ⓑ Süleymaniye
- ⓒ Grand Bazaar
- ⓓ Taj Mahal

6. What leader expanded the Ottoman Empire and organized its laws?
- ⓐ Akbar
- ⓑ Süleyman
- ⓒ Shah Jahan
- ⓓ Babur

7. The Grand Bazaar in Istanbul shows us that the Ottoman Turks were very skilled at _____.
- ⓐ war
- ⓑ trade
- ⓒ art
- ⓓ athletics

8. What is the name of the region where the Ottoman Empire started?
   (a) Italian Peninsula
   (b) Iberian Peninsula
   (c) Asia Minor
   (d) North Africa

9. What capital city of the Ottoman Empire was a center of trade during the Renaissance?
   (a) Baghdad
   (b) Rome
   (c) Istanbul
   (d) Venice

10. Which of the following is a picture of the Taj Mahal?

11. Which of the following best describes the Ottoman and Mughal Empires during the Renaissance?
   (a) large, expanding Muslim empires
   (b) small, shrinking Christian empires
   (c) small, shrinking Hindu empires
   (d) large, expanding African empires

12. What Mughal emperor worked hard to make sure people of different religions lived peacefully together?
    ⓐ Süleyman
    ⓑ Shah Jahan
    ⓒ Akbar
    ⓓ Babur

13. What were the two main religions in India during the Renaissance?
    ⓐ Islam and Christianity
    ⓑ Judaism and Hinduism
    ⓒ Christianity and Hinduism
    ⓓ Hinduism and Islam

14. Draw an X on the map below on the Indian subcontinent.

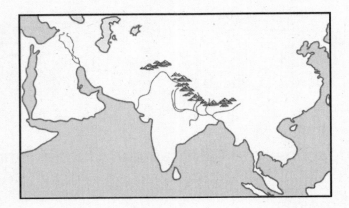

15. This map shows a Muslim empire that grew large and powerful during the time of the Renaissance. Art, literature, and science thrived in this empire. What was it called?

ⓐ the Babylonian Empire
ⓑ the Akbar Empire
ⓒ the Ottoman Empire
ⓓ the Shah Jahan Empire

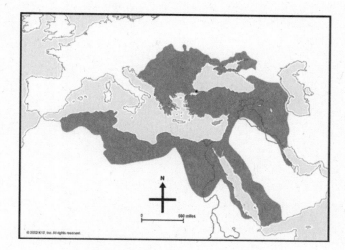

Student Guide
Lesson 1: Benin Grows

- Describe the growth of European trade with Africa, China, and Japan.
- Understand the impact of New World exploration on the development of a transatlantic slave trade.
- Locate on a map the kingdoms of Benin, China, and Japan.
- Recognize that both China and Japan closed themselves to the West in this period.
- Identify key places, dynasties, and products of the three areas: Benin, brasswork, the Niger River, Beijing, the Forbidden City, the Great Wall, the Ming Dynasty, silk and porcelain, the Tokugawa shogunate, and Francis Xavier.

From the mid-1400s to the mid-1600s, the West African kingdom of Benin flourished as a crossroads of trade. Its artisans produced striking sculptures in brass and bronze.

Lesson Objectives

- Describe the growth of European trade with Africa, China, and Japan.
- Understand the impact of New World exploration on the development of transatlantic slave trade.
- Locate on a map the kingdoms of Benin, China, and Japan.
- Recognize that both China and Japan closed themselves to the West in this period.
- Identify key places, dynasties, and products of the three areas: Benin, brasswork, the Niger River, Beijing, the Forbidden City, The Great Wall, The Ming Dynasty, silk and porcelain, the Tokugawa shogunate, and Francis Xavier.
- Locate the kingdom of Benin on a map.
- State that skilled craftsmen in Benin made beautiful works of art from brass.
- Describe the kingdom of Benin as one that flourished because of trade.

PREPARE

Approximate lesson time is 60 minutes.

Materials

For the Student

 Map of Africa, 1600

 globe, inflatable

 History Record Book

 Trading Goods activity sheet

Optional

 Around the World in a Hundred Years: From Henry the Navigator to Magellan by Jean Fritz

Keywords and Pronunciation
Benin (buh-NEEN)
Niger (NIY-jur)
Okoro (oh-KOR-oh)

LEARN
Activity 1: Trade in Benin (Online)

Activity 2: History Record Book (Offline)
Instructions
Choose either A or B.

A. Written Narration
Write two to four sentences explaining what the lesson was about. If necessary, use the Show You Know questions to help get started. Only include the most important parts of the lesson. Write your name, the date, and the lesson title on your written narration, and put it in your History Record Book.

Sample written narration: "Benin was a kingdom in Africa. It was near the Niger River. The people there made beautiful art from brass. They traded with the Portuguese and grew wealthy."

B. Picture Narration
Draw a picture of the part of the lesson that interested you most. When you have finished drawing, describe the picture. Below your picture, write a description of what you have drawn. Write your name, the date, and the lesson title on your picture narration, and put it in your History Record Book.

Activity 3: Goods for Trade (Offline)
Instructions
In the story, Okoro, the king's favorite brass worker, explained that trade with the Portuguese brought great wealth to Benin. Trade usually means that people exchange their goods for goods that others have.

And what are goods? They are things. Goods can be products, like the beautiful brass objects Okoro made. Goods can also be the materials that go into making something else, like the copper and zinc that workers in Benin used to make brass.

Sometimes people exchange goods for money instead of other goods. Then they use the money to buy what they want.

And what is money? It's usually something that people (or a government) agree has value. People agree to accept money as payment, and they also use money as payment. In Benin, people used cowrie shells as money. Think about the last thing you bought. Did you pay for it with money?

Now travel back to Okoro's time and look at the list of goods on the Trading Goods activity sheet. Which ones came from Benin and which ones came from Portugal? After you sort them out, think about some of the goods you have bought and list them. How many cowrie shells do you think they would be worth?

ASSESS

Lesson Assessment: Benin Grows (*Online*)

You will complete an offline assessment covering the main objectives of this lesson. Your learning coach will score this assessment.

LEARN

Activity 4. Optional: Benin Grows (*Offline*)

Instructions

Review the journeys of Prince Henry's sailors and the Portuguese explorer Bartolomeu Dias. Read chapters about them in *Around the World in a Hundred Years: From Henry the Navigator to Magellan,* written by Jean Fritz and illustrated by Anthony Bacon Venti (New York: Putnam, 1994).

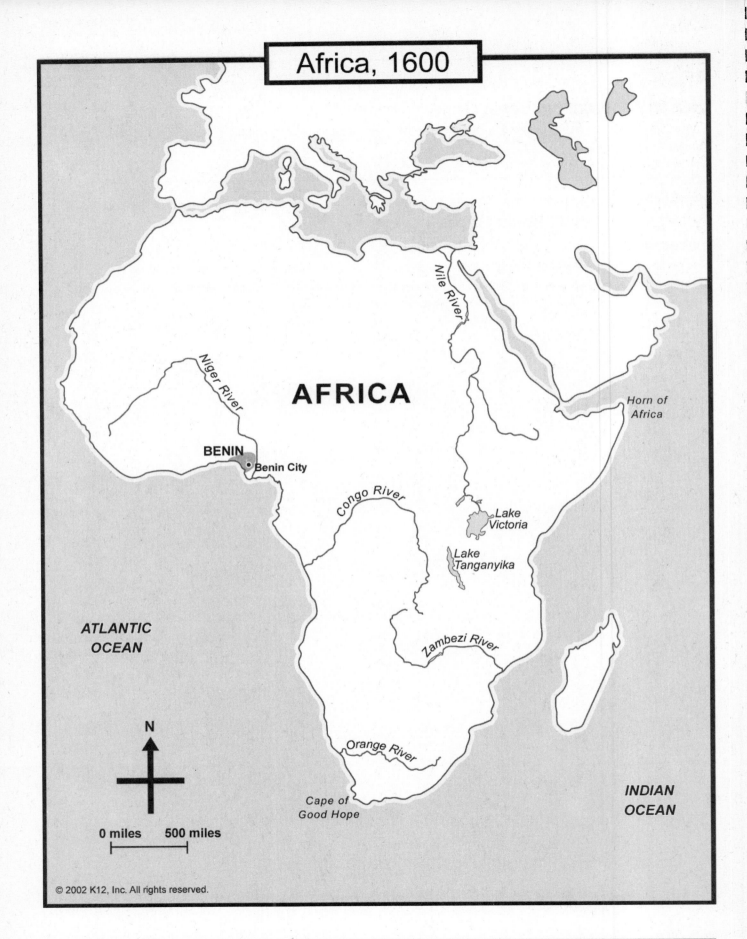

Africa, 1600

AFRICA

Nile River

Niger River

BENIN
• Benin City

Congo River

Lake Victoria

Lake Tanganyika

Horn of Africa

Zambezi River

ATLANTIC OCEAN

Orange River

Cape of Good Hope

INDIAN OCEAN

N

0 miles   500 miles

Name _____   Date _____

Goods for Trade

Here is a list of goods. Some are from the Portuguese. Some are from the kingdom of Benin. Decide where each item belongs and write it under that place. Then think of some goods that you have used money to buy. Write the names of five of those goods in the last column.

1. brass sculptures
2. mirrors
3. gold
4. bronze plaques
5. cowrie shells

6. velvet cloth
7. glass beads
8. ivory
9. coral necklaces
10. candied lemons

Goods from Portugal	Goods from Benin	Goods I've Bought

Lesson Assessment

Benin Grows

1. **In order to answer this question you will need to use the map of Africa, 1600.**

   Where is the kingdom of Benin?

2. In Benin, skilled craftsmen made beautiful sculptures. What metal did they often use to make their

   sculptures?_____

3. How did the kingdom of Benin become rich?_____

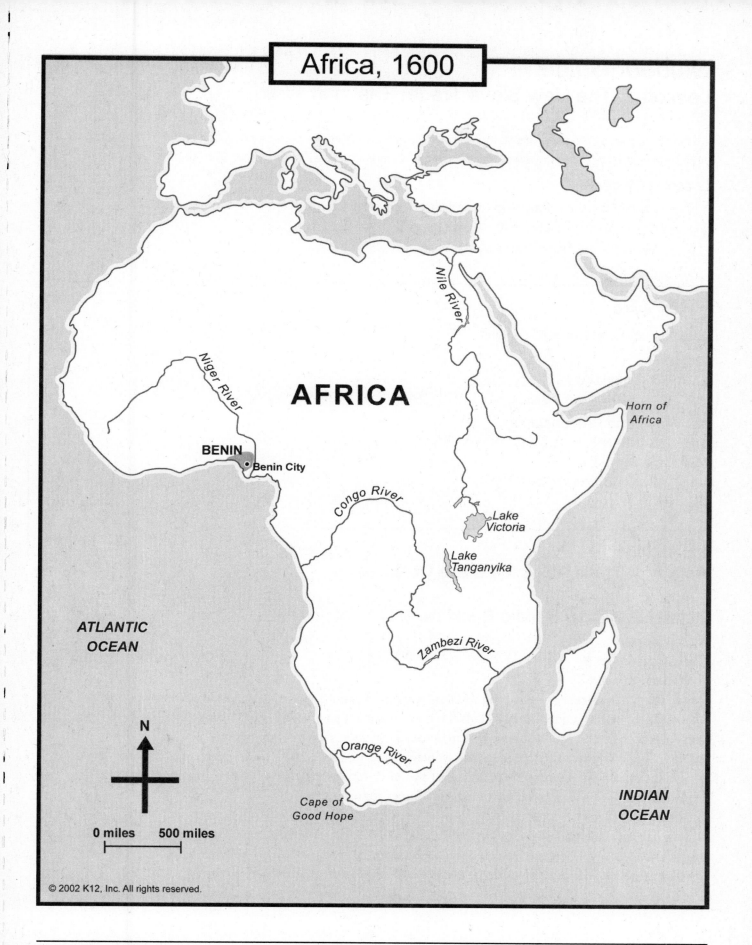

Africa, 1600

AFRICA

Nile River

Niger River

BENIN

Benin City

Congo River

Horn of
Africa

Lake
Victoria

Lake
Tanganyika

Zambezi River

ATLANTIC
OCEAN

Orange River

N

Cape of
Good Hope

INDIAN
OCEAN

0 miles   500 miles

Student Guide
Lesson 2: The New Slave Trade: East and West

As the Portuguese colonized Brazil, the demand for labor to work the sugar plantations grew. Benin and other western African kingdoms grew wealthy by selling Africans as slaves to the eager Portuguese.

Lesson Objectives
- Explain that the Portuguese wanted slaves to work on sugar plantations in the New World.
- Define *transatlantic* to mean "across the Atlantic Ocean."
- Explain some major effects of the transatlantic slave trade.

PREPARE

Approximate lesson time is 60 minutes.

Materials
> For the Student
>> History Record Book

Keywords and Pronunciation
Benin (buh-NEEN)
Mali (MAH-lee)
Mansa Musa (MAHN-sah moo-SAH)
Niger (NIY-jur)

LEARN
Activity 1: Trade Along the Slave Coast *(Online)*

Activity 2: History Record Book *(Offline)*
Instructions
Choose either A or B.

A. Written Narration
Write two to four sentences explaining what the lesson was about. If necessary, use the Show You Know questions to help get started. Only include the most important parts of the lesson. Write your name, the date, and the lesson title on your written narration, and put it in your History Record Book.

Sample written narration: "The Portuguese wanted slaves to work on their sugar plantations in Brazil. They bought them from the rulers of Benin and other people in Africa. They carried slaves across the Atlantic Ocean to Brazil. This was called the transatlantic slave trade."

B. Picture Narration
Draw a picture of the part of the lesson that interested you most. When you have finished drawing, describe the picture. Below your picture, write a description of what you have drawn. Write your name, the date, and the lesson title on your picture narration, and put it in your History Record Book.

Activity 3: Questioning the Slave Trade (Offline)
Instructions

Ask some questions to help you remember what you learned about the slave trade. Here are a few names and terms used in today's lesson. Your job is to write questions that these words answer.

For example, for the first word, *Benin,* you might ask the following question: "What is the name of the kingdom in Africa where the Portuguese began trading for slaves?"

Think of one question for each of the following answers. Then write it on an index card. Write the answer on the back. Then shuffle the cards, read each question, and see if you can remember what you learned about the new slave trade.

1. Benin
2. Brazil
3. gold
4. Portugal
5. slavery
6. the Slave Coast
7. sugar
8. slave traders
9. the transatlantic slave trade

If you can think of even more answers and questions, add them to your list.

ASSESS

Lesson Assessment: The New Slave Trade: East and West (*Online*)

You will complete an offline assessment covering the main objectives of this lesson. Your learning coach will score this assessment.

LEARN

Activity 4. Optional: The New Slave Trade: East and West (Offline)
Instructions

The slave trade spread to South America during the 1500s. What is the name of the large coastal country where slaves helped grow and harvest sugar? Find it on the map. [3]

What is the name of the ocean along this country's coastal border? [4]

The last part of the lesson reminded you about a priest from Spain named Bartolomé de las Casas. Find Spain on the map. What large country forms part of its northern border? [5]

You've learned that Bartolomé de las Casas was against mistreating the native people in the West Indies and Mexico. Find Mexico on the map. Today, what country borders Mexico to the north? [6]

During the time of the slave trade, many Africans were carried across the large ocean that washes up on the shores of Europe, Africa, North America, and South America. What is the word that describes travel across this body of water? [8]

Lesson Assessment

The New Slave Trade: East and West

1. Why did the Portuguese want slaves?_____

2. What does transatlantic mean?_____

3. What happened to the people who were captured as

   slaves?_____

4. Did the people who traded slaves grow rich, or did they find it hard to make money by trading for

   human beings?_____

Student Guide
Lesson 3: The Ming Dynasty and a Forbidden City

Founded by a peasant turned rebel, China's Ming dynasty expelled Mongol conquerors and ushered in a golden age of Chinese culture. The Forbidden City became the symbol of the Ming's power.

Lesson Objectives

- Describe the Ming as an important Chinese dynasty.
- State that the Ming made Beijing the capital city of China.
- Identify the Forbidden City as the home of the emperor.
- List some features of the Forbidden City (such as red brick walls; yellow tile roofs; dragons or animal guardians on roofs).

PREPARE

Approximate lesson time is 60 minutes.

Materials

For the Student
- Map of China and Japan, 1400-1500
- globe, inflatable
- History Record Book
- The Forbidden City activity sheet
- pencils, colored 12

Keywords and Pronunciation

Beijing (bay-zhing)

dynasty : Rule by one family.

lacquered (LA-kurd)

Mongols (MAHNG-guhls)

Mughal (MOO-guhl)

Ottoman (AH-tuh-muhn)

porcelain : A type of hard translucent pottery.

Süleyman (suhlay-MAHN)

Taizu (tiy-dzoo)

Yongle (yohng-lou)

LEARN
Activity 1: The Forbidden City (Online)

Activity 2: History Record Book (Offline)
Instructions
Choose either A or B.
A. Written Narration
Write two to four sentences explaining what the lesson was about. If necessary, use the Show You Know questions to help get started. Only include the most important parts of the lesson. Write your name, the date, and the lesson title on your written narration, and put it in your History Record Book.
Sample written narration: "The Ming dynasty was a powerful family that ruled China. The emperor had a huge palace in Beijing. He called it the Forbidden City. It had stone dragons to guard the palace."
B. Picture Narration
Draw a picture of the part of the lesson that interested you most. When you have finished drawing, describe the picture. Below your picture, write a description of what you have drawn. Write your name, the date, and the lesson title on your picture narration, and put it in your History Record Book.

Activity 3: Using a Map of the Forbidden City (Offline)
Instructions
Retrace your steps through the Forbidden City by using a map and answering some questions. As you tour, think about the name "Forbidden City." The last question will ask you to explain this powerful name.

ASSESS
Lesson Assessment: The Ming Dynasty and a Forbidden City (Online)
You will complete an offline assessment covering the main objectives of this lesson. Your learning coach will score this assessment.

LEARN
Activity 4. Optional: The Ming Dynasty and a Forbidden City (Online)
Now take a virtual tour of the Forbidden City.

Name _____   Date _____

The Forbidden City

Use the map to help you review some of the information you learned about the Forbidden City.

1. Remember that a person who called himself the Son of Heaven gave you a tour of the Forbidden City. What was his name?
    A. Sulee
    B. Mongle
    C. Taizu
    D. Yongle

2. This emperor was a ruler in the _____ dynasty.
    A. Tang
    B. Lacquer
    C. Ming
    D. Porcelain

3. The larger city that is home to the Forbidden City became the capital of China. It is still the capital today. What is its name?
    A. Mongolia
    B. Beijing
    C. Ottoman
    D. Taizuwan

4. In the story, the tour started at the Gate of Supreme Harmony. Think about what the word *harmony* means. What are some other words you could use in its place? Write down one meaning of the word *harmony* before you move on. Then circle or highlight the Gate of Supreme Harmony on the map.

Name _____   Date _____

5.   Next you entered the Hall of Supreme Harmony. Color that area purplish red or dark red. Remember that purple meant "center of the universe," which is what the emperor called himself. Why do you think he thought he was the center of the universe?

6.   On the tour you skipped the Hall of Medium Harmony, so cross it out lightly with a pencil. Then move on to the Hall of Protective Harmony. What do you think the emperor protected here? Perhaps his 25 jade seals for official papers? Draw a small jade seal on the map to help you remember.

7.   Then you went outside to the Hall of Earthly Peace. What are the names of two other places shown on this map on the way to the Hall of Earthly Peace?

8.   Next you visited a place with trees and other plants. It was called the _____.

9.   Finally, you went through one last gate. It's called the Gate of Divine Prowess on this map, but the emperor called it the Gate of Divine Might in the story. He said that he, the Son of Heaven, was both _____ and _____, so the gate really told you about him.

10. Now you've reviewed your visit to the Forbidden City, so you'll need to answer one last question. Why was it called the Forbidden City?

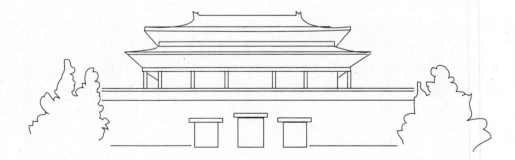

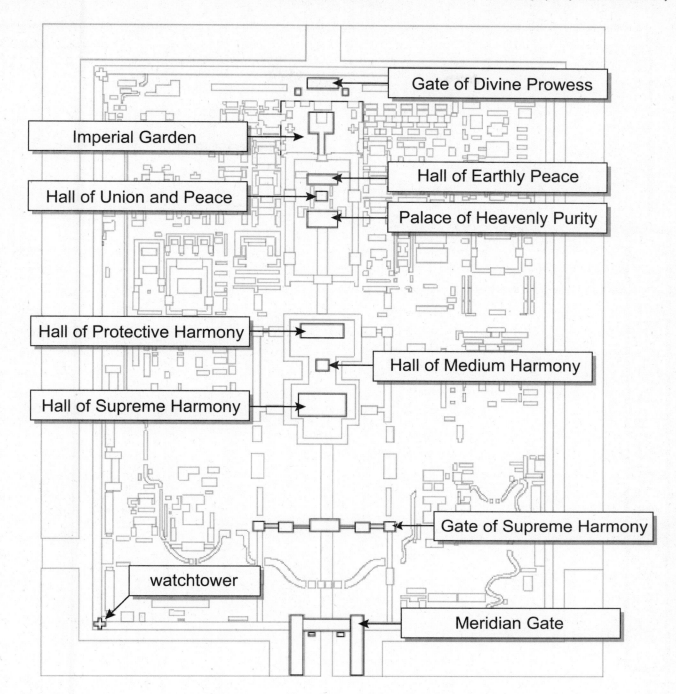

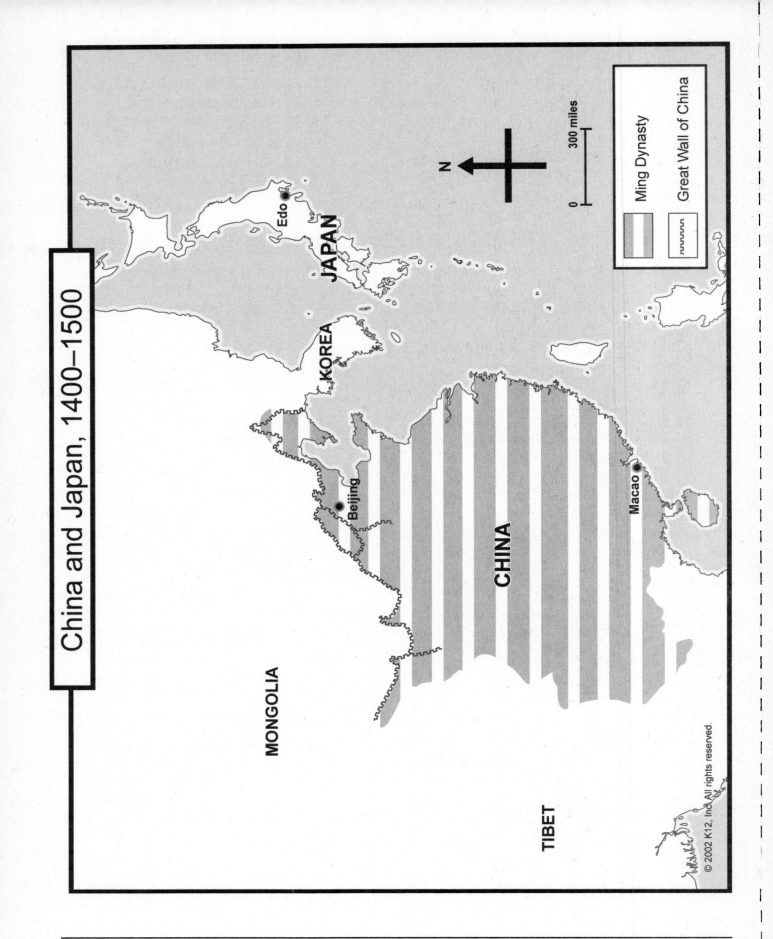

China and Japan, 1400–1500

N

300 miles

0

Ming Dynasty

Great Wall of China

JAPAN

Edo

KOREA

Beijing

CHINA

Macao

MONGOLIA

TIBET

Lesson Assessment

The Ming Dynasty and a Forbidden City

1. Who were the Ming?_____

2. What city did the Ming make the capital of China?_____

3. What was the Forbidden City?_____

4. Describe at least two characteristics of the Forbidden City?_____

    _____

Student Guide
Lesson 4: Chinese Trade in the Age of Exploration

During the Ming dynasty, the Chinese developed a brisk trade with the Spanish and Portuguese in exchange for treasures from the New World. The Chinese traded their silk and porcelain for silver and sweet potatoes from the Americas.

Lesson Objectives

- Describe Zheng He as a Chinese explorer.
- Explain that the Chinese were suspicious of the Europeans.
- Explain that Spain and Portugal began to trade with China.
- List silk and porcelain as goods produced and traded by China.

PREPARE

Approximate lesson time is 60 minutes.

Materials

For the Student

- Map of China and Japan, 1400-1500
- globe, inflatable
- History Record Book
- Resources for Making Silk activity sheet
- pencils, colored 12

Keywords and Pronunciation

Macao (muh-KOW)

porcelain : A type of hard translucent pottery.

Yongle (yohng-lou)

Zheng He (choung hou)

LEARN
Activity 1: Trading Silk and Porcelain (Online)

Activity 2: History Record Book (Offline)

Instructions

Choose either A or B.

A. Written Narration

Write two to four sentences explaining what the lesson was about. If necessary, use the Show You Know questions to help get started. Only include the most important parts of the lesson. Write your name, the date, and the lesson title on your written narration, and put it in your History Record Book.

Sample written narration: "The Chinese did not trust the people who came from Europe to trade. The emperors were worried that the Europeans would try to take over. They let the Portuguese and Spanish trade in one place. The people in Europe wanted silk and porcelain from China."

B. Picture Narration

Draw a picture of the part of the lesson that interested you most. When you have finished drawing, describe the picture. Below your picture, write a description of what you have drawn. Write your name, the date, and the lesson title on your picture narration, and put it in your History Record Book.

Activity 3: Learning More About the Language of Trade (Offline)

Instructions

Trade between China, Spain, and Portugal involved many different goods. China traded silk and porcelain for silver, sweet potatoes, corn, and peanuts. Each of these goods involved different kinds of resources. To produce silk and porcelain, the Chinese used natural, human, and capital resources. Let's look at what happened when the potters of the Ming dynasty made porcelain.

They started with a natural resource--one that occurred in nature. It was a special kind of white clay.

Then they added another kind of resource--a human one. Human resources are the labor, or work, that people add to a natural resource as they make a product. In this case, the clay had to be carefully shaped by a potter using a potter's wheel.

Potter's wheel? That was the tool that helped the Chinese potters turn their natural resource of clay into the beautiful product called porcelain, or china. The potter's wheel was a capital resource. Capital resources are goods that are used to make other goods.

So the Chinese used three kinds of resources to make porcelain:

1. Natural resource: clay
2. Human resource: the person who shaped the clay
3. Capital resource: the potter's wheel used to shape the clay

Now let's see whether you can identify the resources used to make silk. Print the Resources for Making Silk activity sheet and identify the natural, capital, and human resources used to make it.

ASSESS

Lesson Assessment: Chinese Trade in the Age of Exploration (Online)

You will complete an offline assessment covering the main objectives of this lesson. Your learning coach will score this assessment.

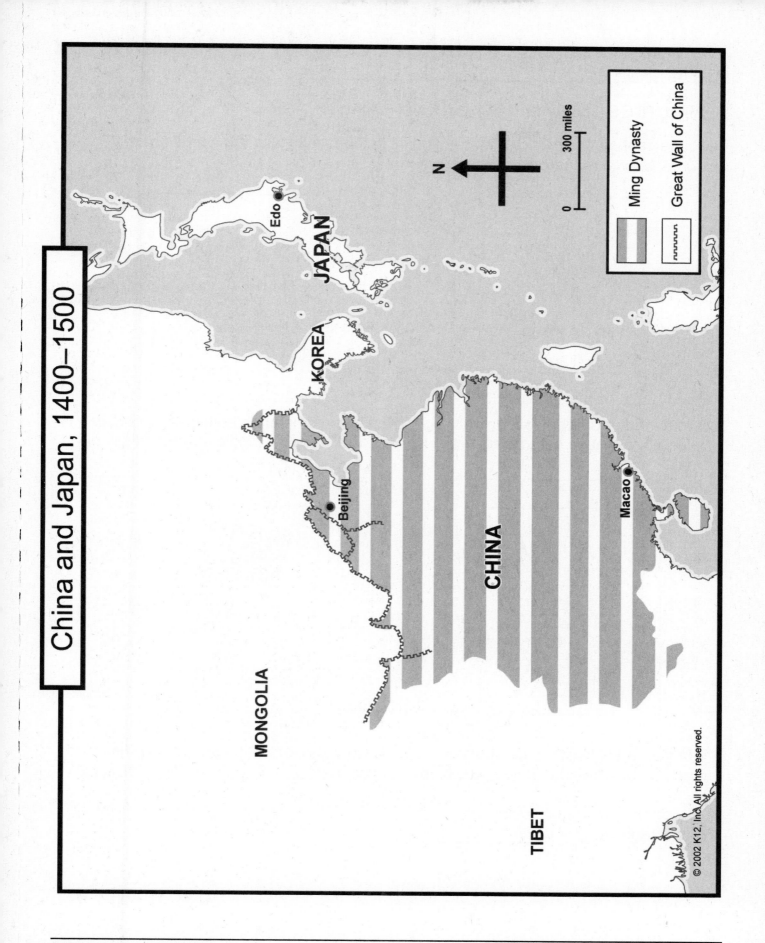

China and Japan, 1400–1500

N

300 miles

0

Ming Dynasty

Great Wall of China

MONGOLIA

TIBET

CHINA

Beijing

KOREA

JAPAN

Edo

Macao

© 2002 K12, Inc. All rights reserved.

Name _____   Date _____

Resources for Making Silk

Read the captions below the pictures and fill in the blanks with the words *natural resource*, *capital resource*, or *human resource*.

1. Silk is made from the cocoons of caterpillars. These caterpillars are a

_____.

2. This woman has boiled each cocoon and is pulling single strands of silk out.

Her work is a _____.

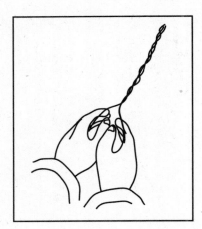

3. The woman is twisting the strands together into threads. She is providing

a _____.

The thread is a _____.

4. Now she is using a tool to help her weave the threads into silk cloth. This

tool is a _____.

Lesson Assessment

Chinese Trade in the Age of Exploration

1. Who was Zheng He?_____

2. What did the Ming emperors think of the Europeans?_____

3. Name two European countries that began to trade with China at that time?_____

4. What two products did everyone want to buy from the Ming in China?_____

Student Guide
Lesson 5: Rebuilding the Great Wall

The Ming emperors built the Great Wall of China to protect their country from Mongol invaders from the north. This monumental wall stretches for thousands of miles and continues to amaze anyone who sees it.

Lesson Objectives

- Explain that the Ming built the Great Wall to keep out invaders.
- Identify the Great Wall of China from photographs.
- Name some characteristics of the Great Wall (for example, it was very long, was made of stone, had watchtowers and signal towers, and was wide enough to fit six horses across).

PREPARE

Approximate lesson time is 60 minutes.

Materials

For the Student

- Map of China and Japan, 1400-1500
  History Record Book
- Great Wall of China activity sheet

Keywords and Pronunciation

Beijing (bay-zhing)
Mongols (MAHNG-guhls)
Taizu (tiy-dzoo)

LEARN
Activity 1: A Look at the Great Wall *(Online)*

Activity 2: History Record Book *(Offline)*

Instructions

Choose either A or B.

A. Written Narration

Write two to four sentences explaining what the lesson was about. If necessary, use the Show You Know questions to help get started. Only include the most important parts of the lesson. Write your name, the date, and the lesson title on your written narration, and put it in your History Record Book.

Sample written narration: "The Chinese wanted to keep the Mongols out of their empire. They already had a Great Wall, but it was old and falling down. So the Ming decided to rebuild the Great Wall. They had signal towers to light fires and tell soldiers when they were being attacked."

B. Picture Narration

Draw a picture of the part of the lesson that interested you most. When you have finished drawing, describe the picture. Below your picture, write a description of what you have drawn. Write your name, the date, and the lesson title on your picture narration, and put it in your History Record Book.

Activity 3: Painting the Great Wall *(Offline)*
Instructions
Do you remember the soldier you met on the Great Wall? He said that the Mongols didn't write poems or paint pictures as the Chinese did.

Use watercolor paint to add color to the Great Wall of China activity sheet. Then write three to five sentences to finish a paragraph that describes the Great Wall. If you're having trouble thinking of sentences that describe the Great Wall, revisit the Reading Room and read the story again.

ASSESS
Lesson Assessment: Rebuilding the Great Wall (*Online*)
You will complete an offline assessment covering the main objectives of this lesson. Your learning coach will score this assessment.

LEARN
Activity 4. Optional: Rebuilding the Great Wall *(Online)*
Visit the Great Wall of China without leaving your home!

Name _____   Date _____

Great Wall of China

Use watercolor paint to add color to the drawing below. Then write three to five sentences that describe the Great Wall.

The Great Wall of China is an amazing structure. _____

_____

_____

_____

_____

_____

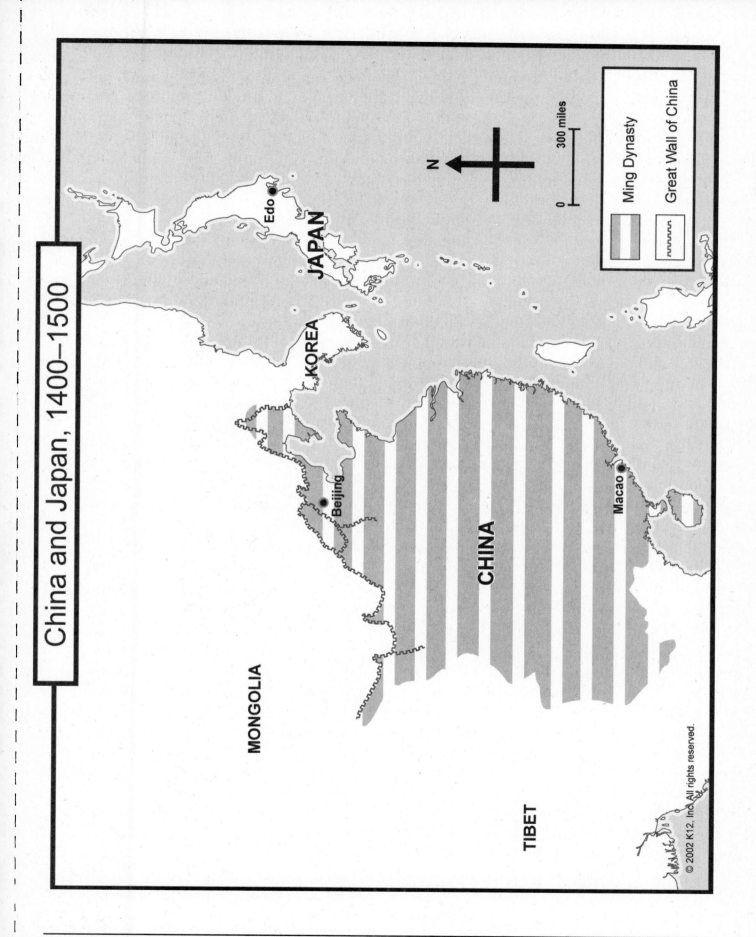

China and Japan, 1400–1500

MONGOLIA

TIBET

CHINA

KOREA

JAPAN

Beijing

Macao

Edo

N

300 miles

0

Ming Dynasty

Great Wall of China

© 2002 K12, Inc. All rights reserved.

Name_____   Date_____

Lesson Assessment

Rebuilding the Great Wall

1. Why did the Ming rebuild the Great Wall?_____

2. What is shown in this picture?_____

3. What are some of the features you remember about the Great Wall?_____

_____

Student Guide
Lesson 6: The Portuguese in Feudal Japan

East of China lay the island kingdom of Japan. When the Portuguese arrived in Japan in the 1500s, they found a land of warring samurai.

Lesson Objectives

- Describe Japan as an island kingdom.
- Recognize that people in Japan lived under a feudal system.
- Describe the period in which the Portuguese arrived as a time of fighting.
- Explain that the Portuguese went to Japan to trade and to spread the Christian faith.

PREPARE

Approximate lesson time is 60 minutes.

Materials

For the Student

- 🖳 Map of China and Japan, 1400-1500
  - History Record Book
  - crayons 8
  - paper, 8 1/2" x 11"
  - pencils, colored 12

Keywords and Pronunciation

Buddha (BOO-duh)
Buddhism (BOO-dih-zuhm)
daimyos (DIY-mee-ohs)
Francis Xavier (ZAYV-yur)
samurai (SA-muh-riy)
shogun (SHOH-guhn) : The chief military ruler of Japan.

LEARN
Activity 1: The Portuguese in Feudal Japan (Online)

Activity 2: History Record Book (Offline)

Instructions
Choose either A or B.

A. Written Narration
Write two to four sentences explaining what the lesson was about. If necessary, use the Show You Know questions to help get started. Only include the most important parts of the lesson. Write your name, the date, and the lesson title on your written narration, and put it in your History Record Book.

Sample written narration: "Japan was a place where warriors called samurai fought with sharp swords. They fought with each other a lot. The Portuguese ships came to Japan to trade for silver and gold. They sent missionaries to teach people about Christianity."

B. Picture Narration
Draw a picture of the part of the lesson that interested you most. When you have finished drawing, describe the picture. Below your picture, write a description of what you have drawn. Write your name, the date, and the lesson title on your picture narration, and put it in your History Record Book.

Activity 3: Trading Begins in Feudal Japan (Offline)
Try your hand at creating a banner carrying a message about trade.

ASSESS
Lesson Assessment: The Portuguese in Feudal Japan (Online)
You will complete an offline assessment covering the main objectives of this lesson. Your learning coach will score this assessment.

LEARN
Activity 4. Optional: The Portuguese in Feudal Japan (Online)
Look at a map online to learn more about the island kingdom of Japan.

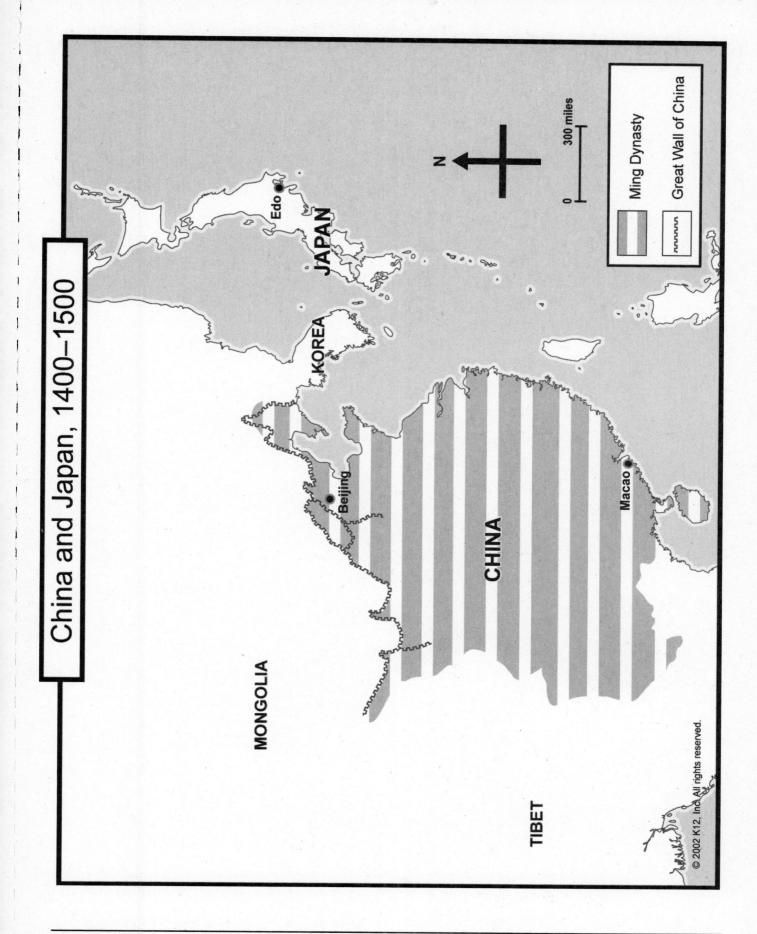

China and Japan, 1400–1500

N

300 miles

0

Ming Dynasty

Great Wall of China

MONGOLIA

KOREA

JAPAN

Edo

Beijing

TIBET

CHINA

Macao

© 2002 K12, Inc. All rights reserved.

Name _____   Date _____

Lesson Assessment Key

The Portuguese in Feudal Japan

1. Would you describe Japan as one large landmass or a kingdom of many islands?_____

2. What kind of system did the Japanese have to rule and protect themselves?_____

3. When the Portuguese arrived in Japan, were the Japanese at peace or at war among themselves?_____

4. Give two reasons why the Portuguese sent ships to Japan?_____

Student Guide
Lesson 7: The Tokugawa Shoguns Throw the Foreigners Out

The powerful Tokugawa family rose to power and its leaders became shoguns of Japan. At first they encouraged trade with Europeans, but then decided Japan would be better off without foreigners. Eventually they expelled Europeans, closing Japan off from the rest of the world.

Lesson Objectives

- Define *shogun* as the chief military ruler of Japan.
- Recognize that the Tokugawa were powerful rulers of Japan.
- Explain that early Tokugawa shoguns expelled Europeans from Japan.

PREPARE

Approximate lesson time is 60 minutes.

Materials

> For the Student
> > History Record Book
> > paper, notebook

Keywords and Pronunciation

Edo (AY-doh)

shogun (SHOH-guhn) : The chief military ruler of Japan.

Tokugawa Ieyasu (toh-kou-GAH-wuh ee-YAY-uhs)

LEARN
Activity 1: The Tokugawa Shoguns Expel Foreigners *(Online)*

Activity 2: History Record Book *(Offline)*
Instructions

Choose either A or B.

A. Written Narration

Write two to four sentences explaining what the lesson was about. If necessary, use the Show You Know questions to help get started. Only include the most important parts of the lesson. Write your name, the date, and the lesson title on your written narration, and put it in your History Record Book.

Sample written narration: "The Tokugawa were a powerful family of rulers in Japan. They were the shoguns. They decided that foreigners were bad for Japan. They threw all the foreigners out."

B. Picture Narration

Draw a picture of the part of the lesson that interested you most. When you have finished drawing, describe the picture. Below your picture, write a description of what you have drawn. Write your name, the date, and the lesson title on your picture narration, and put it in your History Record Book.

Activity 3: The News About the Tokugawa Shogunate (Offline)
Instructions
When television or newspaper reporters prepare their stories, they try to answer these important questions:

- Who?
- What?
- Where?
- When?
- Why?
- How?

Now it's your turn to try your hand as a reporter. Decide whether you want to prepare a television or newspaper report. Your topic is Tokugawa Japan. You have either three minutes on the air or one page in print to deliver your information.

Answer the questions first. Then write your script or article. Share your work with someone else.

ASSESS

Lesson Assessment: The Tokugawa Shoguns Throw the Foreigners Out
(*Online*)
You will complete an offline assessment covering the main objectives of this lesson. Your learning coach will score this assessment.

LEARN
Activity 4. Optional: The Tokugawa Shoguns Throw the Foreigners Out (Online)
What do you think was happening in Tokugawa Japan while it was closed to foreigners? Check out an art exhibit to see for yourself.

Lesson Assessment

The Tokugawa Shoguns Throw the Foreigners Out

1. What was a shogun?_____

2. We learned about a family in Japan called the Tokugawa. Who were the

    Tokugawa?_____

3. What did the Tokugawa do to foreigners?_____

Student Guide
Lesson 8: Unit Review and Assessment

You've completed this unit, and now it's time to review what you've learned and take the unit assessment.

Lesson Objectives

- Demonstrate mastery of important knowledge and skills in this unit.
- Locate the kingdom of Benin on a map.
- State that skilled craftsmen in Benin made beautiful works of art from brass.
- Explain that the Portuguese wanted slaves to work on sugar plantations in the New World.
- Explain some major effects of the transatlantic slave trade.
- State that the Ming made Beijing the capital city of China.
- Identify the Forbidden City as the home of the emperor.
- List some features of the Forbidden City (such as red brick walls; yellow tile roofs; dragons or animal guardians on roofs).
- Explain that Spain and Portugal began to trade with China.
- List silk and porcelain as goods produced and traded by China.
- Explain that the Ming built the Great Wall to keep out invaders.
- Name some characteristics of the Great Wall (for example, it was very long, was made of stone, had watchtowers and signal towers, and was wide enough to fit six horses across).
- Recognize that people in Japan lived under a feudal system.
- Describe the period in which the Portuguese arrived as a time of fighting.
- Recognize that the Tokugawa were powerful rulers of Japan.
- Explain that early Tokugawa shoguns expelled Europeans from Japan.

PREPARE

Approximate lesson time is 60 minutes.

Materials

> For the Student
>> History Record Book

Keywords and Pronunciation

Benin (buh-NEEN)

daimyos (DIY-mee-ohs)

Francis Xavier (ZAYV-yur)

Mongols (MAHNG-guhls)

Niger (NIY-jur)

samurai (SA-muh-riy)

shogun (SHOH-guhn) : The chief military ruler of Japan.

Tokugawa (toh-kou-GAH-wuh)

LEARN
Activity 1: A Look Back (Offline)
Instructions

We've learned about a kingdom that flourished in Africa and powerful dynasties that ruled China and Japan. And we've seen how East and West met each other as never before.

Let's review. In Africa during the 1500s, the kingdom of Benin grew. Do you remember where Benin was located? [1] The craftsmen of Benin created beautiful brass pieces for their altars and palaces. Brass work was a royal art. But when the Portuguese found the kingdom of Benin, they weren't interested in brass. They wanted to trade for Benin's spices and ivory. So Portugal and Benin became trading partners. It wasn't long before Portugal wanted to trade for something else, too. Do you remember what else the Portuguese wanted? [2]

Why did the Portuguese want African slaves? [3]

The rulers of Benin sold African prisoners to the Portuguese as slaves. A new slave trade began. There had been a slave trade throughout the Middle Ages. But this trade was different. In the next few hundred years, millions of Africans would be taken from their homes and sent across the Atlantic Ocean to labor in the New World. It made Benin, other African kingdoms, and European traders rich. And it created a huge injustice in the New World. For centuries African slavery would become a way of life in the Americas.

In China, the Ming dynasty came to power in the 1300s and ruled over a golden age that lasted almost 300 years. *Ming* means "bright," and the accomplishments of the Chinese during this period were very bright. They wove fine silk and shaped handsome blue-and-white porcelain dishes. They traded their famous silk and porcelain for potatoes and silver from the New World. Their population grew and grew.

The Ming worried about foreigners--especially the pesky Mongols to the north. The Ming emperor decided to move the capital city of China north to Beijing. He ordered workers to build an imperial palace, a fabulous city within a city. China's Forbidden City became home to China's royal family. Why was it called the Forbidden City? [4] The Forbidden City's mighty red walls and yellow-tiled roofs announced the splendor and power of the Ming.

The Ming showed their splendor and power in other ways, too. The Ming emperor decided China needed even more protection from the Mongols. So he decided to rebuild the Great Wall. The Ming got hundreds of thousands of men to build a wall that stretched 1,500 miles across northern China. It had watchtowers and walkways wide enough to ride six horses side by side. Visitors still walk along parts of the Great Wall today.

East of China lay the island kingdom of Japan. In 1500 the Japanese had a feudal system, much like Europe during the Middle Ages. Landowning nobles were protected by warriors, who were like knights. Do you remember what Japan's noble lords were called? [5] What were the warriors who protected them called? [6] In the early 1500s those lords and samurai were fighting each other. A huge civil war raged in Japan. In a way, the Europeans ended it.

The Europeans arrived in Japan unexpectedly. They were interested in spreading Christianity and trade. Do you remember the name of the Jesuit priest who came to spread Christianity in Japan? [7] Father Francis admired the Japanese people. He converted some Japanese to the Catholic faith. The Japanese admired one thing about the Europeans--their guns! When the daimyos traded with the Europeans for guns, one strong family finally took over. What was the name of the family whose leaders became powerful shoguns in Japan? [8]

It didn't take long for the Tokugawa to grow suspicious of the Europeans. They didn't like the new Christian faith, and they didn't trust the Europeans. Eventually the Tokugawa killed the Japanese who had converted to Christianity, and threw the Europeans out.

By 1600 the world was becoming connected as never before. Portuguese and Spanish merchants had succeeded in their quest to reach the Indies. They established ports wherever they went. Sometimes they were welcomed. Sometimes they were thrown out. But in Africa, China, and Japan, the Portuguese and Spanish found people and treasures that would change the world.

Other European nations didn't want to be left behind in this race to explore and colonize. England would soon set out upon the seas and challenge Portugal and Spain. But that's our next story!

Activity 2: History Record Book Review (Offline)

Use the contents of your History Record Book to review the unit on Africa, China, and Japan. Take some time to revisit the narrations, activity sheets, writing activities, and pictures in the History Record Book. Read the narrations aloud. Don't hurry this part of the review; it will refresh your memory and give you a sense of just how much you've already learned.

Instructions

Use the contents of your History Record Book to review the unit on Africa, China, and Japan. Take some time to revisit the narrations, activity sheets, writing activities, and pictures in the History Record Book. Read the narrations aloud. Don't hurry this part of the review; it will refresh your memory and give you a sense of just how much you've already learned.

Activity 3: Online Interactive Review (Online)

ASSESS

Unit Assessment: Africa, China, and Japan (Offline)

Complete an offline Unit Assessment. Your learning coach will score this part of the Assessment.

Name _____ Date _____

Africa, China, and Japan

Read each question and its answer choices. Fill in the bubble in front of the word or words that best answer the question.

Questions marked with an asterisk (*) will have more than one correct answer. For these questions, fill in the bubble next to ALL correct answers.

1. Skilled craftsmen in the African kingdom of Benin made beautiful works of art out of what material?
   - (a) iron
   - (b) brass
   - (c) silver
   - (d) porcelain

2. Why did the Portuguese want slaves?
   - (a) to build merchant ships
   - (b) to train as soldiers
   - (c) to work on sugar plantations
   - (d) to make artwork for their king

3. What city became the capital of the Ming dynasty?
   - (a) Istanbul
   - (b) Beijing
   - (c) Baghdad
   - (d) Tokyo

* 4. What two goods were produced and traded by China? (Select two that are correct.)
   - ⓐ silver
   - ⓑ silk
   - ⓒ guns
   - ⓓ mirrors
   - ⓔ porcelain

5. Why did the Ming build the Great Wall of China?
   - ⓐ to keep invading armies out
   - ⓑ to keep peasants from leaving
   - ⓒ to protect traveling merchants
   - ⓓ to divide the country into two parts

6. People in Japan lived under a _____ system, in which they exchanged work for protection.
   - ⓐ feudal
   - ⓑ slave
   - ⓒ Christian
   - ⓓ Buddhist

7. What strong family rose to power to become shoguns in Japan?
   - ⓐ Ming
   - ⓑ Ottoman
   - ⓒ Tokugawa
   - ⓓ Mughal

8. How did the transatlantic slave trade affect the kingdom of Benin?
   - (a) The Portuguese conquered the kingdom.
   - (b) Benin became smaller and poorer.
   - (c) The leaders of Benin began exploring.
   - (d) Benin grew and became wealthier.

9. What is the main reason that the transatlantic slave trade began?
   - (a) The Chinese built the Great Wall to keep invaders out of China.
   - (b) The Portuguese began exploring and farming in South America.
   - (c) The Japanese shoguns threw Europeans out of Japan.
   - (d) The Portuguese began trading with China and Japan.

* 10. Four of the following are features of the Forbidden City. Select any two that are correct.
   - (a) red brick walls
   - (b) stained glass windows
   - (c) yellow tile roofs
   - (d) wide domes
   - (e) tall spires
   - (f) sculpted stone staircases
   - (g) dragons or animals on the roof

* 11. Which two European countries led the Age of Exploration and were the first to start trading with China and Japan? (Select two that are correct.)
   - (a) England
   - (b) France
   - (c) Spain
   - (d) Portugal

12. What was happening in Japan when the Portuguese arrived?
    ⓐ One powerful shogun ruled over a peaceful kingdom.
    ⓑ Daimyos and samurai were fighting to gain power.
    ⓒ The Japanese were sending ships to explore China.
    ⓓ Japanese merchants were buying slaves in Africa.

13. What did Japanese rulers do when they began to fear and distrust foreign ideas and religion?
    ⓐ They talked to their advisors and decided from the votes of wise men.
    ⓑ They built a long wall to keep Europeans out.
    ⓒ They made Europeans leave Japan and persecuted Christians.
    ⓓ They traded silk for slaves in Africa.

14. Write each of the following words in the column where it belongs.

Ming dynasty Tokugawa shogunate Forbidden City
spices and ivory Beijing feudal system slave trade

Benin	China	Japan
brass art	Great Wall	Edo
	silk and porcelain	

15. Describe the Great Wall of China. (Name at least three of its characteristics.)

_____

_____

_____

16. True or False: Europeans were able to visit and trade with China and Japan all through the Renaissance.

   ○ True

   ○ False

17. Locate the kingdoms of Benin, China, and Japan on the following maps by labeling Benin "B", China "C," and Japan "J."15

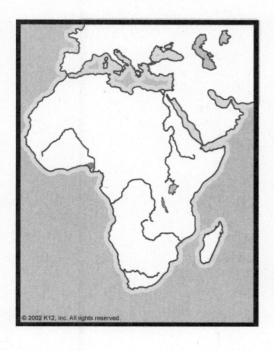 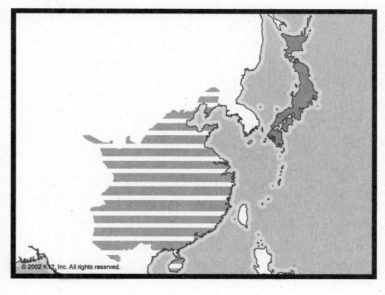

Student Guide
Lesson 1: Elizabeth I: Her Father's Daughter

- Identify the reign of Elizabeth as a "golden age," or time of cultural and political flourishing.
- Identify England as an increasingly strong nation-state under Elizabeth I.
- Identify Spain as England's main rival.
- State that England began to explore and colonize North America.
- Identify Shakespeare as England's most famous bard.
- Recognize historic English concern for defense of liberties in the quarrel with James I and the Glorious Revolution.

Elizabeth I, the intelligent, strong-willed daughter of Henry VIII, made England a powerful and culturally vibrant nation. Visit England during her reign, which lasted nearly 50 years and is known as the golden age of England.

Lesson Objectives

- Identify the reign of Elizabeth as a "golden age," or time of cultural and political flourishing.
- Identify England as an increasingly strong nation-state under Elizabeth I.
- Identify Spain as England's main rival.
- State that England began to explore and colonize North America.
- Identify Shakespeare as England's most famous bard.
- Recognize historic English concern for defense of liberties in the quarrel with James I and the Glorious Revolution.
- Describe Elizabeth I as a great English queen.
- Name two problems England faced when Elizabeth was crowned (religious splits within England, rivalry with Spain, people not used to rule by a woman).
- Define the expression "golden age" as a high point of learning and accomplishment.
- Define the expression "Elizabethan era" as the time when Elizabeth I was queen of England.
- State that England became a powerful nation under Elizabeth's rule.

PREPARE

Approximate lesson time is 60 minutes.

Materials

For the Student

    History Record Book

    pencils, colored 12

Optional

    Good Queen Bess: The Story of Elizabeth I of England by Diane Stanley and Peter Vennema

Keywords and Pronunciation

coronation : Ceremony at which a king or queen is crowned.

LEARN
Activity 1: Elizabeth I: The Start of a Golden Age *(Online)*

Activity 2: History Record Book *(Offline)*
Instructions
Choose either A or B.
A. Written Narration
Write two to four sentences explaining what the lesson was about. If necessary, use the Show You Know questions to help get started. Only include the most important parts of the lesson. Write your name, the date, and the lesson title on your written narration, and put it in your History Record Book.

Sample written narration: "Elizabeth I was the daughter of Henry VIII. Elizabeth grew up to be queen. The people of England were not used to being ruled by a woman, but Elizabeth was a strong queen. When she ruled, it was called the golden age of England."

B. Picture Narration
Draw a picture of the part of the lesson that interested you most. When you have finished drawing, describe the picture. Below your picture, write a description of what you have drawn. Write your name, the date, and the lesson title on your picture narration, and then put it in your History Record Book.

Activity 3: Come to the Coronation! *(Offline)*
Instructions
The coronation of Elizabeth I as queen of England must have been a spectacular affair! This daughter of Henry VIII was strong and smart like her father. She would need her strength and intelligence in the years ahead to prove that a woman could rule a country. The English people seemed ready to give her a chance. Create a poster announcing the coronation of Elizabeth I. While you design the poster, keep in mind that this is only the beginning of her reign. You wouldn't know yet that England would become a powerful nation under her rule. You also wouldn't know that she would become a great English queen.

However, include information about some of the problems England faced when Elizabeth was crowned. Suggest that she will be able to help solve these problems.

ASSESS
Lesson Assessment: Elizabeth I: Her Father's Daughter *(Online)*
You will complete an offline assessment covering the main objectives of this lesson. Your learning coach will score this assessment.

LEARN
Activity 4. Optional: Elizabeth I: Her Father's Daughter *(Offline)*
Instructions

Check your library or bookstore for *Good Queen Bess: The Story of Elizabeth I of England*, by Diane Stanley and Peter Vennema (New York: Four Winds Press, 1990).

This wonderfully illustrated biography of Good Queen Bess (Elizabeth I) covers the conflict between Catholics and Protestants and gives information about Elizabeth's greatest challenges as queen.

Name _____ Date _____

Lesson Assessment

Elizabeth I: Her Father's Daughter

1. Name the daughter of Henry VIII who became a great English queen. _____

2. Name two problems England faced when Elizabeth became queen? _____

3. What do we call a time in a country's history that is a high point of learning and accomplishment? _____

4. Elizabeth's reign began a golden age in England. Historians have given this era in English history a special name. What was this name? _____

5. Did England become weaker under Elizabeth's rule or more powerful? _____

Student Guide
Lesson 2: Sir Francis Drake

English sea captain and pirate Sir Francis Drake helped make England a sea power that rivaled Spain and Portugal. His voyage around the world established a British presence in the Pacific.

Lesson Objectives

- Name Spain and Portugal as England's major rivals during the Renaissance.
- Describe Francis Drake as a daring English sea captain who attacked Spanish and Portuguese ships.
- State that Francis Drake made a voyage around the world.

PREPARE

Approximate lesson time is 60 minutes.

Materials

For the Student

    globe, inflatable

    History Record Book

    🖳 Sir Francis Drake Goes to Sea activity sheet

    index cards

    tape, clear

Keywords and Pronunciation

circumnavigation : To go completely around the world by water.

Gibraltar (juh-BRAWL-tuhr)

LEARN
Activity 1: Drake Sails the Seas for Elizabeth I *(Online)*

Activity 2: History Record Book *(Offline)*

Instructions

Choose either A or B.

A. Written Narration

Write two to four sentences explaining what the lesson was about. If necessary, use the Show You Know questions to help get started. Only include the most important parts of the lesson. Write your name, the date, and the lesson title on your written narration, and put it in your History Record Book.

Sample written narration: "Francis Drake went to sea with his ship, the Golden Hind. He was looking for Spanish treasure ships. He got a lot of treasure. Then he sailed around the world back to England."

B. Picture Narration

Draw a picture of the part of the lesson that interested you most. When you have finished drawing, describe the picture. Below your picture, write a description of what you have drawn. Write your name, the date, and the lesson title on your picture narration, and then put it in your History Record Book.

Activity 3: Sir Francis Drake Goes to Sea *(Offline)*

Instructions

Sir Francis Drake sailed his ship, the *Golden Hind,* west across the Atlantic Ocean, through the Strait of Magellan, and into the Pacific. Then he turned north and followed the west coast of South America, attacking Spanish ships and settlements along the way.

After capturing a Spanish ship laden with treasure, Drake decided it was time for the *Golden Hind* to return to England. But he couldn't turn back and sail east through the Strait of Magellan--Spanish ships would be waiting to attack him.

Instead, Drake sailed west, crossing the Pacific and Indian Oceans. He rounded the Cape of Good Hope and sailed north, returning to England.

Create small labels (about 1/2" × 2") from 3" × 5" index cards with the following names: Plymouth, England; English Channel; Atlantic Ocean; Strait of Magellan; equator; Pacific Ocean; Indian Ocean; Cape of Good Hope.

Tape these labels in the appropriate places on the globe. Now take a length of yarn or string and tape it to the globe so that it shows Drake's route around the world. Use the map of Drake's Voyage Around the World as a reference.

Now complete the Sir Francis Drake Goes to Sea activity sheet by adding one or two entries to the log of the *Golden Hind.* You may want to read the story again to review the facts about Drake's voyage around the world.

ASSESS

Lesson Assessment: Sir Francis Drake (*Online*)

You will complete an offline assessment covering the main objectives of this lesson. Your learning coach will score this assessment.

Name   Date

Sir Francis Drake Goes to Sea

Captains kept written records of their voyages in a ship's log, or logbook. Two events described in the *Golden Hind's* logbook for Drake's circumnavigation are given below. Complete one or two entries for an event (or events) that would have occured between the two described below.

Log of the Golden Hind

March 1, 1579

Took the Cacafuego. 80 pounds of gold, 13 chests of coins, 26 tons of silver, and cases of jewels and pearls. Also captured a pilot.

_____

_____

_____

_____

_____

_____

_____

September 26, 1580

Return to Plymouth. Wondering...is the queen still alive?

Lesson Assessment

Sir Francis Drake

1. What two countries were England's major rivals? _____

2. Who was Sir Francis Drake? _____

3. How did Sir Francis Drake help make England rich and

   powerful? _____

4. Where had Drake sailed by the time he got back to England? _____

Student Guide
Lesson 3: Defeat of the Spanish Armada

England's defeat of the "invincible" Spanish fleet signaled the rise of a new power in Europe.

Lesson Objectives

- Define *Spanish Armada* as a fleet of armed Spanish ships.
- State that Sir Francis Drake and the English navy defeated the Spanish Armada in 1588.
- Explain that England became a major sea power as a result of its defeat of the Spanish Armada.

PREPARE

Approximate lesson time is 60 minutes.

Materials

For the Student

    globe, inflatable

    History Record Book

    🖳 A Famous Sea Battle activity sheet

    glue, children's white

    pencils, colored 12

    scissors

Keywords and Pronunciation

armada : A fleet of warships.
Armada (ahr-MAH-duh)

LEARN
Activity 1: England Defeats the Spanish Armada (Online)

Activity 2: History Record Book (Offline)
Instructions

Choose either A or B.

A. Written Narration

Write two to four sentences explaining what the lesson was about. If necessary, use the Show You Know questions to help get started. Only include the most important parts of the lesson. Write your name, the date, and the lesson title on your written narration, and put it in your History Record Book.

Sample written narration: "The Spanish sent a great fleet to defeat England. It was called the Spanish Armada. The English ships beat the Spanish Armada. England became a great sea power after that."

B. Picture Narration

Draw a picture of the part of the lesson that interested you most. When you have finished drawing, describe the picture. Below your picture, write a description of what you have drawn. Write your name, the date, and the lesson title on your picture narration, and then put it in your History Record Book.

Activity 3: A Famous Sea Battle (Offline)
Instructions
After defeating Spain's "invincible" fleet, the Spanish Armada, England became a major sea power. This means that the English navy became larger and more powerful. With a larger navy, England could protect its merchant ships as they plied the trade routes between Europe and the Indies. As a result, England became wealthier.

Follow the directions on the Famous Sea Battle activity sheet to reenact this famous sea battle.

ASSESS
Lesson Assessment: Defeat of the Spanish Armada (Online)
You will complete an offline assessment covering the main objectives of this lesson. Your learning coach will score this assessment.

A Famous Sea Battle

Activity Preparation

1. Color the flags of England and Spain. The background of the English flag is white, and the cross is red. The background of the Spanish flag is red, and the cross is gold. Cut the flags out and glue each one to a craft stick.

2. Color ship banners for the two fleets, cut them out, and glue each one to a toothpick.

3. Color Sir Francis Drake and Philip II, cut them out, and glue each one to a craft stick.

4. Make small bases out of clay, and stick each craft stick into a base.

5. Mold six small, simple ships out of clay.

Reenacting the Battle

1. Place the flags of England and Spain on the countries where they belong.

2. Place Francis Drake and Philip II on the countries where they belong.

3. Place four ships, representing the Spanish Armada, on the map off the coast of northern Spain. Put them in a crescent formation: Stick the banner for the Spanish Armada in one of the ships.

4. Place two ships, representing the English navy, off the coast of England near Plymouth Harbor. Stick the banner for the English navy in one of the ships.

5. Now move the ships to reenact the battle. Describe what is happening. Review the story if necessary to help you recall the sequence of events.

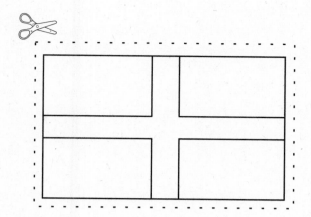

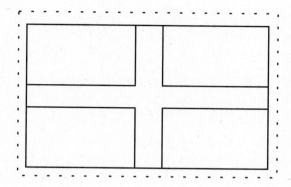

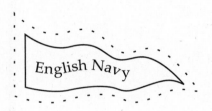

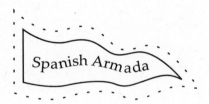

Francis Drake

Philip II

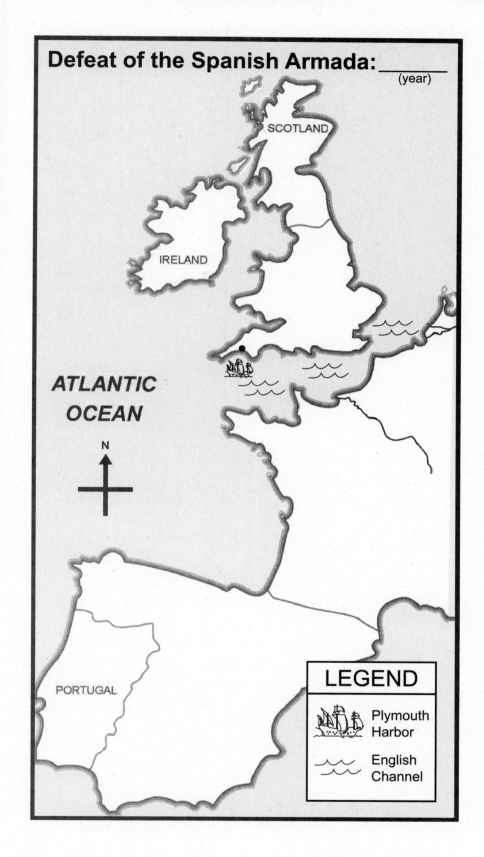

Defeat of the Spanish Armada: _____
(year)

SCOTLAND

IRELAND

ATLANTIC OCEAN

N

PORTUGAL

LEGEND

Plymouth Harbor

English Channel

Lesson Assessment

Defeat of the Spanish Armada

1. What was the Spanish Armada?_____

2. What great English explorer and sea captain fought the Spanish Armada?_____

3. Did the Spanish Armada succeed in conquering England in 1588?_____

4. Did England become a great sea power after the defeat of the Spanish Armada, or did it become a weaker sea power?_____

Student Guide
Lesson 4: Go Forth, Sir Walter!

Another favorite of Queen Elizabeth, Sir Walter Raleigh was a soldier, explorer, and poet. Raleigh offered to help establish colonies in North America. Although he failed, he began a process England would continue.

Lesson Objectives
- Name Walter Raleigh as the first person to attempt settlement of English colonies in North America.
- Describe Walter Raleigh as a person who was interested in exploration.
- Name Roanoke as the Lost Colony.

PREPARE

Approximate lesson time is 60 minutes.

Materials
    For the Student
        map, world
        History Record Book
    Optional
        The Lyon's Roar by M.L. Stainer

Keywords and Pronunciation
El Dorado (el duh-RAH-doh)

LEARN
Activity 1: A Courtier with a Thirst for Adventure *(Online)*

Activity 2: History Record Book *(Offline)*
Instructions

Choose either A or B.

A. Written Narration
Write two to four sentences explaining what the lesson was about. If necessary, use the Show You Know questions to help get started. Only include the most important parts of the lesson. Write your name, the date, and the lesson title on your written narration, and put it in your History Record Book.

Sample written narration: "Queen Elizabeth liked Sir Walter Raleigh. He wanted to explore and sail across the sea. He sent ships to America, but they became the Lost Colony. Sir Walter Raleigh sailed to South America looking for gold."

B. Picture Narration
Draw a picture of the part of the lesson that interested you most. When you have finished drawing, describe the picture. Below your picture, write a description of what you have drawn. Write your name, the date, and the lesson title on your picture narration, and then put it in your History Record Book.

Activity 3: Sir Walter Raleigh Arrives at Court *(Offline)*
Instructions

As one of Queen Elizabeth's favorite courtiers, Sir Walter Raleigh would make many a grand entrance at court functions. When important guests arrived at court, it was someone's job to stand at the entrance to the room and loudly announce the name of each person arriving.

Write an announcement for Sir Walter Raleigh. Imagine he is making his entrance at the court of Queen Elizabeth. You know that he's one of the queen's favorites, so you want to say more than just his name. Include some information that shows how important he is.

For example:

- He's an explorer, a poet, a patriot, and a soldier.
- He's witty and intelligent.
- He's gallant--he laid his new cloak down on a mud puddle so the queen wouldn't get her shoes dirty.
- He organized the first attempts to establish settlements in North America.
- He led an expedition to South America to search for El Dorado.

After you write the announcement, practice reading it aloud. Then make the announcement in front of an audience. Speak loudly and clearly; add some flair to your little speech!

ASSESS

Lesson Assessment: Go Forth, Sir Walter! *(Online)*

You will complete an offline assessment covering the main objectives of this lesson. Your learning coach will score this assessment.

LEARN
Activity 4. Optional: Go Forth, Sir Walter! *(Offline)*
Instructions

The story of the Lost Colony is a fascinating one. To learn more about this attempt to establish a permanent English colony in the New World, search the Internet for websites about Roanoke and the Lost Colony.

For a great book on the subject, check your library or bookstore for *The Lyon's Roar,* written by M.L. Stainer and illustrated by James Melvin (Circleville, NY: Chicken Soup Press, 1997). This novel, the first of five books in a series that covers 25 years of America's earliest colonial history, tells the story of the failed attempt to establish a settlement on Roanoke Island.

Name _____   Date _____

Lesson Assessment

Go Forth, Sir Walter!

1. Who was the first person to try to set up English colonies in North America? _____

2. When Raleigh was at court, what did he miss being able to do? _____

3. Name Raleigh's most famous colony in the New World. It became known as the Lost

   Colony. _____

Student Guide
Lesson 5: Shakespeare: England's Bard

The greatest playwright who ever wrote in the English language, William Shakespeare was a man of enterprise and insight. This glove-maker's son wrote at least 38 plays, influenced theater around the world, and gave the English language many of its frequently used expressions.

Lesson Objectives

- Name William Shakespeare as the greatest English poet and playwright.
- State that William Shakespeare wrote many plays during the Elizabethan era.
- Give two English expressions we still use that come from Shakespeare's plays.

PREPARE

Approximate lesson time is 60 minutes.

Materials
    For the Student
        History Record Book
        🖳 To Coin a Phrase activity sheet
        pencils, colored 12

Keywords and Pronunciation
playwright : A person who writes plays.

LEARN
Activity 1: A Writer for All Time (Online)

Activity 2: History Record Book (Offline)
Instructions

Choose either A or B.

A. Written Narration
Write two to four sentences explaining what the lesson was about. If necessary, use the Show You Know questions to help get started. Only include the most important parts of the lesson. Write your name, the date, and the lesson title on your written narration, and put it in your History Record Book.

Sample written narration: "William Shakespeare wrote plays better than anyone else in England. He went to London and became famous. We still use some of the words he wrote, like *shooting star* and *bump.* People still like his plays a lot."

B. Picture Narration
Draw a picture of the part of the lesson that interested you most. When you have finished drawing, describe the picture. Below your picture, write a description of what you have drawn. Write your name, the date, and the lesson title on your picture narration, and then put it in your History Record Book.

Activity 3: Shakespeare's Contributions to the Language *(Offline)*

Instructions

Hundreds of years after Shakespeare's time, English-speaking people still use his words and expressions. Explore some of the more famous ones on the To Coin a Phrase activity sheet. The third expression appears in a sentence, giving an example of how it might be used.

After reading and discussing some of Shakespeare's contributions to the English language, choose two words or expressions. Write them at the bottom of the activity sheet, and then come up with a definition or meaning for each word or expression. Write a sentence using these words or expressions. If you have time, draw a picture that helps illustrate the meaning of each word or expression.

ASSESS

Lesson Assessment: Shakespeare: England's Bard (*Online*)

You will complete an offline assessment covering the main objectives of this lesson. Your learning coach will score this assessment.

Name _____   Date _____

To Coin a Phrase

Read these words and expressions that William Shakespeare invented. Discuss their meanings. Choose two, write them below, and give a definition for each. Use each one in a sentence. Try drawing a picture that helps explain its meaning.

budge an inch	dead as a doornail	tower of strength
green-eyed (with jealousy)	gloomy	fair play
tongue-tied	eyesore	the long and short of it
knit your brow	a laughingstock	excellent
It's Greek to me	lovely	lie low
hoodwinked	slept not one wink	suspect foul play
in a pickle	It's high time	without rhyme or reason

Example:

Word/Expression: _tongue-tied_____

Meaning: _Can't think what to say._____

Sentence: _When the teacher asked him a question, he was _tongue-tied_._____

1. Word/Expression: _____

Meaning: _____

_____

Sentence: _____

_____

2. Word/Expression: _____

Meaning: _____

_____

Sentence: _____

_____

Lesson Assessment

Shakespeare: England's Bard

1. Who was the greatest English poet and playwright?_____

2. What did Shakespeare write that made him so famous?_____

3. During what time in England's history did Shakespeare write his plays?_____

4. Name two English expressions or words we still use that come from Shakespeare's

   plays._____

Student Guide
Lesson 6. Optional: All the World's a Stage: The Globe

At the height of his success, Shakespeare became part-owner of the Globe, London's new theater in the round. Nearly all of his plays premiered there, delighting as many as 3,000 people at each performance.

Lesson Objectives

- Name the Globe as the London theater where Shakespeare's plays were performed.
- Describe the Globe as a theater in the round that was open to the sky.
- Tell two characteristics of Elizabethan theatergoers and theater.

PREPARE

Approximate lesson time is 60 minutes.

Materials

    For the Student

        History Record Book

        📖 Globe Theatre Model activity sheet

        glue, children's white

        pencils, colored 12

        scissors

        tape, clear

LEARN
Activity 1. Optional: Optional Lesson Instructions (Online)

This lesson is OPTIONAL. It is provided for students who seek enrichment or extra practice. You may skip this lesson.

If you choose to skip this lesson, then go to the Plan or Lesson Lists page and mark this lesson "Skipped" in order to proceed to the next lesson in the course.

Activity 2. Optional: Theater in the Elizabethan Era (Online)

Activity 3. Optional: History Record Book (Offline)

Instructions

Choose either A or B.

A. Written Narration

Write two to four sentences explaining what the lesson was about. If necessary, use the Show You Know questions to help get started. Only include the most important parts of the lesson. Write your name, the date, and the lesson title on your written narration, and put it in your History Record Book.

Sample written narration: "The theater where William Shakespeare put on his plays was called the Globe. It was round. The groundlings sat on the ground to watch and only had to pay a penny. They threw apples when they didn't like the show."

B. Picture Narration

Draw a picture of the part of the lesson that interested you most. When you have finished drawing, describe the picture. Below your picture, write a description of what you have drawn. Write your name, the date, and the lesson title on your picture narration, and put it in your History Record Book.

Activity 4. Optional: Make a Model of the Globe (Online)

Make a paper model of the Globe Theatre.

Activity 5. Optional: All the World's a Stage: The Globe (Online)

Take a tour of the Globe Theater!

Globe Theatre Model

1. Print two copies of this activity sheet—one to cut up and one for reference. When you have completed this model, none of the tabs should show.

2. If you'd like to add color to your Globe Theatre, visit the websites in the Beyond the Lesson activity that offer virtual tours of the Globe. Do this before assembling your model. Use colored pencils or markers to add color. For example, you could color the roof panels brown.

3. Cut out each part along the dotted lines.

   Parts to cut out:

   - Outside walls 1 and 2
   - Inside walls 1 and 2
   - Two entranceways
   - Stage

4. Cut the short dotted lines along the edge of each outside wall so there is a row of tabs along the top of the wall. These are the roof panels.

5. Glue tab A on the right edge of outside wall 1 to the left edge of outside wall 2 to form one combined outside wall.

6. Glue tab B on the right edge of inside wall 1 to the left edge of inside wall 2 to form one combined inside wall.

7. Fold the two entranceways and glue the tabs at the roof. Don't glue the entranceways to the theater building itself until step 12.

8. Fold the stage and glue the tabs.

9. Turn the combined outside wall face down. Glue the back of the combined inside wall (face up) onto the back of the combined outside wall (face down). Do not glue the ½ inch on the left because you will need to insert tab C between the inside and outside walls in the next step.

10. Bring the combined strip around in a circle so that the inside wall is on the inside and the outside wall is on the outside. Glue both sides of tab C and insert the tab between the inside and outside walls.

11. Bend the roof panels in toward the inside walls.

12. On both entranceways, fold each tab D in and glue it to the outside wall where it is indicated.

13. Place the stage inside, opposite the entranceways.

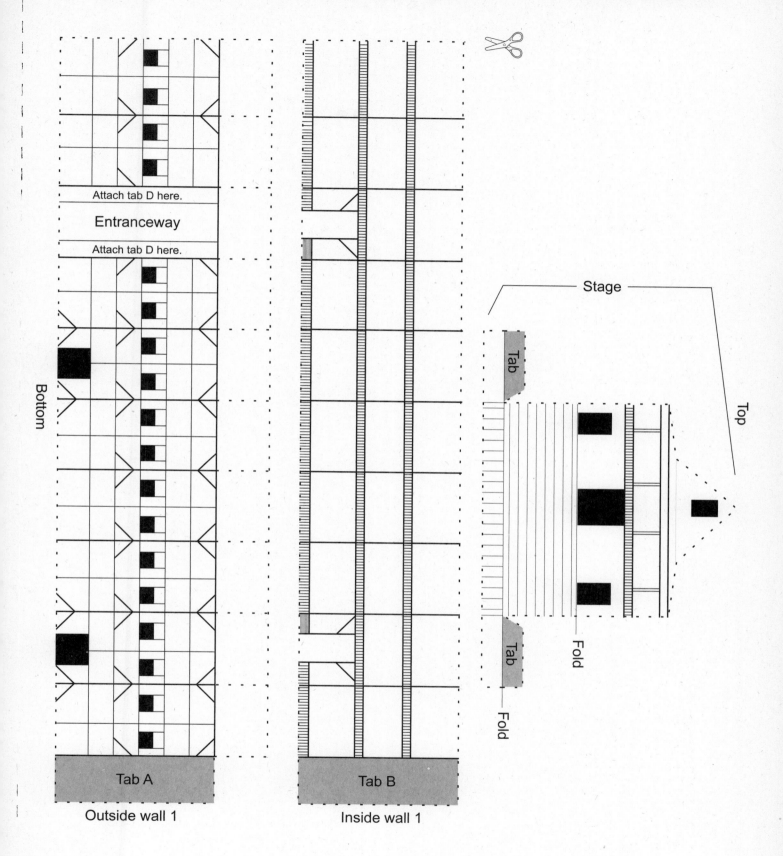

Attach tab A to this end.

Attach tab B to this end.

Tab D

Tab D

Entranceway

Top

Tab D

Tab D

Entranceway

Bottom

Attach tab D here

Entranceway

Attach tab D here

Tab C

Outside wall 2

Inside wall 2

Student Guide
Lesson 7: Stewing the Stuarts

When Elizabeth died leaving no heirs, the English throne passed from the Tudors to their cousins, the Stuarts. The Stuarts believed in divine right of kings and failed to consult Parliament, the lawmaking body of the English government. Parliament ousted the Stuarts in a civil war, and England briefly became a republic.

Lesson Objectives

- State that the Stuart dynasty succeeded the Tudors.
- Identify James I as the king of Scotland and the monarch who succeeded Elizabeth.
- Define "divine right of kings" as the belief that kings got their authority from God and not from the people.
- Explain that Parliament ousted the Stuarts.

PREPARE

Approximate lesson time is 60 minutes.

Materials
For the Student
    History Record Book
    📖 No to Divine Right activity sheet

Keywords and Pronunciation

divine right : The belief that a monarch received authority to rule directly from God and not from the people.

English Parliament (PAHR-luh-muhnt) : The lawmaking body of England, including representatives of the nobility and of the commoners.

LEARN
Activity 1: Divine Right, Divine Wrong *(Online)*

Activity 2: History Record Book *(Offline)*
Instructions
Choose either A or B.

A. Written Narration

Write two to four sentences explaining what the lesson was about. If necessary, use the Show You Know questions to help get started. Only include the most important parts of the lesson. Write your name, the date, and the lesson title on your written narration, and put it in your History Record Book.

Sample written narration: "James I was a Stuart. He believed in the divine right of kings and argued a lot with Parliament. Parliament went to war with the Stuarts and won."

B. Picture Narration

Draw a picture of the part of the lesson that interested you most. When you have finished drawing, describe the picture. Below your picture, write a description of what you have drawn. Write your name, the date, and the lesson title on your picture narration, and put it in your History Record Book.

Activity 3: Parliament Says "No" to Divine Right (Offline)
Instructions
The Stuarts, and most kings before them, believed that God gave them the right to rule England and its people. This idea is known as "the divine right of kings." By the 1600s, many people in England, including those who served in Parliament, thought that monarchs should get their authority to rule from the people. Complete the No to Divine Right activity sheet to show the differences in how people felt about the divine right of kings.

ASSESS
Lesson Assessment: Stewing the Stuarts (Online)
You will complete an offline assessment covering the main objectives of this lesson. Your learning coach will score this assessment.

LEARN
Activity 4. Optional: Stewing the Stuarts (Offline)
Instructions
It's common for famous people to have other people, places, or things named after them. Remember Ignatius of Loyola? Many colleges and universities are named after him.

King James I also had many things named after him. Perhaps the two that are best known are the Jamestown settlement in Virginia and the King James version of the Bible.

Choose either the Jamestown settlement or the King James Bible as your subject, and do some more research. Go to the public library and look for books on your subject. Try a search on the Internet. Write down facts about your topic. Once you have gathered some information, decide how you would like to present your research findings. You might choose one of these:

- a short written report
- an oral presentation
- a visual presentation (poster, diorama, etc.)

Name _____ Date _____

Parliament Says "No" to Divine Right

What would the Stuarts have said about how kings should rule? What would Parliament have said? Write the sentences from the box below in the section where they belong.

The Stuarts say...

_____

_____

_____

_____

_____

Parliament says...

_____

_____

_____

_____

_____

"Kings are God's representatives on earth."

"Kings should obey the laws of Parliament."

"I can't believe my ancestors allowed Parliament to exist."

"A king is free to do as he wants."

"Kings receive their authority to rule from the English people."

"Kings rule in the place of God on earth."

"Kings have some rights, but Parliament has rights, too."

Lesson Assessment

Stewing the Stuarts

1. Which family, or dynasty, followed the Tudors? _____

2. Which monarch succeeded, or came after, Elizabeth? _____

3. What was the divine right of kings? _____

4. Who won the war between the Stuarts and Parliament? _____

Student Guide
Lesson 8: A Glorious Revolution

The republic in England did not last long. After a period of turmoil, the Stuarts returned to the throne. Then the Glorious Revolution ousted the king, established the supremacy of Parliament, and gave the throne to William and Mary, who signed a Bill of Rights.

Lesson Objectives

- Describe the republic in England as short-lived.
- State that the English Parliament invited William and Mary to rule England.
- Explain that the Glorious Revolution was a bloodless revolution that made Parliament more powerful than the king.
- Explain that with the English Bill of Rights, the king promised to keep the laws made by Parliament.

PREPARE

Approximate lesson time is 60 minutes.

Materials

For the Student

    History Record Book

    🖥 A Century of Turmoil in England activity sheet

    glue, children's white

    pencils, colored 12

    scissors

Keywords and Pronunciation

Glorious Revolution : Bloodless transfer of power to William and Mary, which established the supremacy of Parliament.

Thames (temz)

LEARN
Activity 1: From Divine Right to the Bill of Rights (Online)

Activity 2: History Record Book (Offline)

Instructions

Choose either A or B.

A. Written Narration

Write two to four sentences explaining what the lesson was about. If necessary, use the Show You Know questions to help get started. Only include the most important parts of the lesson. Write your name, the date, and the lesson title on your written narration, and put it in your History Record Book.

Sample written narration: "The English Parliament asked William and Mary to be the king and queen of England. They had to agree to a Bill of Rights. This was called the Glorious Revolution. It meant that now Parliament was really making the laws."

B. Picture Narration

Draw a picture of the part of the lesson that interested you most. When you have finished drawing, describe the picture. Below your picture, write a description of what you have drawn. Write your name, the date, and the lesson title on your picture narration, and put it in your History Record Book.

Activity 3: A Century of Turmoil in England (Offline)
Instructions

A lot happened in England during the 1600s. The Tudor dynasty ended and the Stuarts came to the throne. Stuart monarchs fought with Parliament off and on until Parliament removed them from power. For a while, England had no king. Then the Stuarts returned, but a Glorious Revolution removed them from power once again. The new king and queen agreed to follow the laws that Parliament made.

In the span of one hundred years, England went from a country where kings ruled by divine right to a country where representatives of the nobility and common folk had more power than the king. While all this change was going on, several monarchs sat on the English throne.

Use the Century of Turmoil in England activity sheet to show the monarchs who ruled England and the events that took place during the seventeenth century.

ASSESS

Lesson Assessment: A Glorious Revolution (*Online*)

You will complete an offline assessment covering the main objectives of this lesson. Your learning coach will score this assessment.

LEARN

Activity 4. Optional: A Glorious Revolution (*Online*)

You learned a lot about Parliament in this lesson. Now see where Parliament meets.

Name _____   Date _____

A Century of Turmoil in England

Cut out the portraits of English monarchs on page 3. Glue them in their correct locations on pages 1 and 2. This will show the descriptions of succession of English monarchs during the seventeenth century. Then cut out the six events on page 3 and glue them onto pages 1 and 2 in the order that they occurred.

 *Seventeenth-Century English Monarchs*

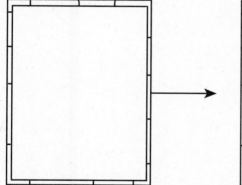 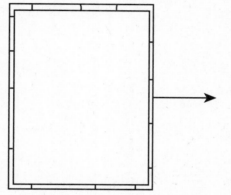 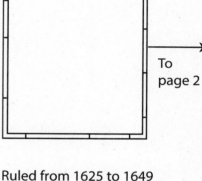

To page 2

Ruled from 1558 to 1603
Last of the House of Tudor

Ruled from 1603 to 1625
Was king of Scotland

Ruled from 1625 to 1649
Son of James I
Fought against Parliament
 in a civil war
Lost his head

Event
1
1603

Event
2
1649

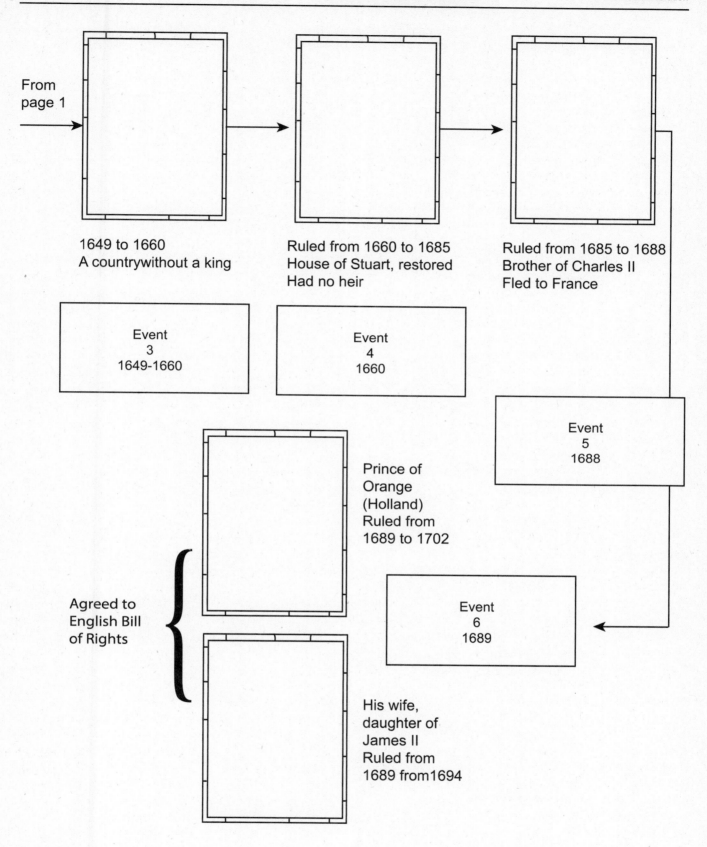

From page 1

1649 to 1660
A countrywithout a king

Ruled from 1660 to 1685
House of Stuart, restored
Had no heir

Ruled from 1685 to 1688
Brother of Charles II
Fled to France

Event
3
1649-1660

Event
4
1660

Event
5
1688

Prince of
Orange
(Holland)
Ruled from
1689 to 1702

Agreed to
English Bill
of Rights

Event
6
1689

His wife,
daughter of
James II
Ruled from
1689 from1694

Rulers

James I

William III

Elizabeth I

Charles II

Parliament

Charles I

James II

Mary II

Events

Parliament dislikes the idea of the "divine right of kings," and gets rid of the Stuarts.

William and Mary agree to the English Bill of Rights.

England becomes a country without a king.

Parliament invites William and Mary to rule England as king and queen.

Charles II assumes the throne and the Stuarts are back in power.

Tudor dynasty ends when James I (a Stuart) becomes king of England after Queen Elizabeth dies.

Lesson Assessment

A Glorious Revolution

1. Did the English republic last a long time or was it short-lived? _____

2. Whom did Parliament invite to rule England during the reign of James II? _____

3. Was the Glorious Revolution bloodless or did it involve a lot of fighting? _____

4. What group became more powerful as a result of the Glorious Revolution? _____

5. What did the king of England promise to do in the Bill of Rights? _____

Student Guide
Lesson 9: Unit Review and Assessment

You've completed this unit, and now it's time to review what you've learned and take the unit assessment.

Lesson Objectives

- Demonstrate mastery of important knowledge and skills in this unit.
- Demonstrate mastery of important knowledge and skills taught in previous lessons.
- Name two problems England faced when Elizabeth was crowned (religious splits within England, rivalry with Spain, people not used to rule by a woman).
- Define the expression "golden age" as a high point of learning and accomplishment.
- Define the expression "Elizabethan era" as the time when Elizabeth I was queen of England.
- State that England became a powerful nation under Elizabeth's rule.
- Describe Francis Drake as a daring English sea captain who attacked Spanish and Portuguese ships.
- Define *Spanish Armada* as a fleet of armed Spanish ships.
- State that Sir Francis Drake and the English navy defeated the Spanish Armada in 1588.
- Name Walter Raleigh as the first person to attempt settlement of English colonies in North America.
- Describe Walter Raleigh as a person who was interested in exploration.
- Name William Shakespeare as the greatest English poet and playwright.
- State that the Stuart dynasty succeeded the Tudors.
- Define "divine right of kings" as the belief that kings got their authority from God and not from the people.
- Explain that the Glorious Revolution was a bloodless revolution that made Parliament more powerful than the king.
- Explain that with the English Bill of Rights, the king promised to keep the laws made by Parliament.

PREPARE

Approximate lesson time is 60 minutes.

Materials

> For the Student
>> History Record Book

Keywords and Pronunciation

Armada (ahr-MAH-duh)

English Parliament (PAHR-luh-muhnt) : The lawmaking body of England, including representatives of the nobility and of the commoners.

Tudor (TOO-dur)

LEARN
Activity 1: A Look Back (Offline)
Instructions

England has had many famous rulers. King Arthur lives in memory. So does King Richard of the Crusades. People remember bad King John of the Magna Carta, and of course King Henry VIII with his many wives and his Church of England. But it was a queen, not a king, who ruled over England's golden age. She was red-haired and strong-willed. She could read Latin and Greek. She was quick-witted and thoughtful. And she made England a powerful nation.

Queen Elizabeth, daughter of Henry VIII, ruled England for nearly 45 years. She ruled while England's navy grew powerful. She ruled while English drama blossomed. She ruled while English merchants and adventurers began to explore the New World.

Let's see if we can remember some of the important people and events during Elizabeth's rule. Here are three: Sir Francis Drake, Sir Walter Raleigh, and the defeat of the Spanish Armada.

What do you remember about Francis Drake and Walter Raleigh? They were English adventurers and pirates. They both started off by raiding Spanish ships. And in 1588 they both fought in the most important naval battle of their age--known ever after as "the defeat of the Spanish Armada."

Why was that defeat so important? At that time Spain and Portugal, great navigators and colonizers, were the richest countries in Europe. Spain had the strongest navy and the largest number of colonies in the New World. Spanish treasure ships bulged with gold and silver from the Americas. They drooped under the weight of gems from the east. Some ambitious Englishmen were not content to watch the Spanish get rich. English pirates ventured into the seas. They attacked Spanish ships and plundered their treasures. Daring men like Drake and Raleigh sent much of their booty back to Queen Elizabeth.

Philip II of Spain was so annoyed at these English pirates that he decided to finish off the pesky island nation of England. So he sent his fleet, the Armada, to invade England. But Elizabeth was ready. With men like Walter Raleigh and Francis Drake as captains, the English navy defeated the Spanish fleet.

That victory signaled the start of a new age of English sea power. English merchants and explorers started mapping the coast of North America. Businessmen began to plan colonies there. Sir Walter Raleigh planned one at Roanoke, but it failed. Later, others would succeed. The English people were very proud and happy. They celebrated Elizabeth and they celebrated life.

What was the best way to celebrate life? Why, watching a play by William Shakespeare, of course! During its golden age, England gave the world its greatest playwright ever: William Shakespeare. He wrote more plays and wrote them more beautifully than any other playwright. Shakespeare wrote about love and pride, ambition and jealousy, and his England, "this precious stone set in the silver sea."

Today people still watch Shakespeare's wonderful plays and use many expressions he gave us. His theater, the Globe, became the center of London social life. The queen, her nobles, and common folk all came to the Globe.

Shakespeare described the English as "this happy breed of men." But when Elizabeth died, the English were not so happy. Gone were the Tudors, the family of Henry and Elizabeth. In came the Stuarts, Elizabeth's cousins. Gone too was Tudor good sense about how kings should act toward Parliament. In came "divine right of kings."

James I and his son, Charles I, thought that God himself had given them the right to rule. The Stuarts didn't much care what members of Parliament thought, and they said so. Nobles and commoners represented in Parliament decided they didn't much care what the Stuarts thought, either. Parliament raised an army. In a big civil war, Parliament beheaded Charles I and set up a republic. That didn't work for very long either, but a big change came as a result.

The English people decided they wanted a king, but a king who respected their rights. So they sent for the Dutch rulers William and Mary. William and Mary were in Holland, but they accepted the English invitation. In England, they signed a Bill of Rights promising to respect the laws made by Parliament.

That change was called the Glorious Revolution. Why was it glorious? Because, without any bloodshed, "divine right" was gone. A Bill of Rights was in. The English had new rulers who gave much more power to Parliament. English kings forever after knew that Parliament, the representative of nobility and common folk, would be supreme.

Activity 2: History Record Book Review (Offline)
Instructions
Use the contents of your History Record Book to review the unit on England's Golden Age and Beyond. Take some time to revisit the narrations, activity sheets, writing activities, and pictures in the History Record Book. Read the narrations aloud. Don't hurry this part of the review; it will refresh your memory and give you a sense of just how much you've already learned.

Activity 3: Online Interactive Review (Online)

ASSESS

Unit Assessment: Unit Review and Assessment (Offline)
Complete an offline Unit Assessment. Your learning coach will score this part of the Assessment.

Name _____   Date _____

England's Golden Age and Beyond

Read each question and its answer choices. Fill in the bubble in front of the word or words that best answer the question.

Questions marked with an asterisk (*) will have more than one correct answer. For these questions, fill in the bubble next to ALL correct answers.

1. Under what great queen did England become a powerful nation?
   - ⓐ Mary III
   - ⓑ Elizabeth I
   - ⓒ Isabella
   - ⓓ Eleanor

2. Who was Francis Drake?
   - ⓐ a French explorer who searched for the Northwest Passage
   - ⓑ an English explorer who started a colony at Roanoke
   - ⓒ a Spanish priest who built missions in South America
   - ⓓ an English sea captain who made a voyage around the world

3. What event occurred in 1588 that made England a major sea power?
   - ⓐ James I became king of England.
   - ⓑ A sea route to the Indies was discovered.
   - ⓒ The English navy defeated the Spanish Armada.
   - ⓓ William and Mary agreed to the Bill of Rights.

4. Who was the first person to attempt to establish a permanent English settlement in North America?
   - ⓐ Walter Raleigh
   - ⓑ William Shakespeare
   - ⓒ James I
   - ⓓ Francis Drake

5. Who was William Shakespeare?
- ⓐ an English explorer and pirate
- ⓑ an English playwright and poet
- ⓒ a French painter and sculptor
- ⓓ a Spanish sea captain and explorer

6. "Divine right of kings" is the belief that kings get their authority to rule from whom?
- ⓐ Parliament
- ⓑ God
- ⓒ the pope
- ⓓ the Church of England

7. Which monarch ruled England during its "golden age"?

Henry VIII

James I

Elizabeth I

Mary II

8. What was England's major rival during the Elizabethan era?
- ⓐ France
- ⓑ Spain
- ⓒ Russia
- ⓓ China

9. England's golden age was a time of learning and accomplishment during whose reign?
- ⓐ Henry VIII
- ⓑ Elizabeth I
- ⓒ James II
- ⓓ William and Mary

10. What did England begin to do during the reign of Elizabeth I?
- ⓐ conquer and rule countries in Asia
- ⓑ explore and colonize North America
- ⓒ build cathedrals and churches in Ireland
- ⓓ explore and colonize South America

11. What was the Spanish Armada?
- ⓐ a fleet of armed Spanish ships that conquered England
- ⓑ soldiers who supported Parliament during England's civil war
- ⓒ a play about Spain's navy written by William Shakespeare
- ⓓ a fleet of armed Spanish ships defeated by the English

* 12. Which of the following are true statements about Walter Raleigh? (Select ALL that are true.)
- ⓐ He experimented with telescopes.
- ⓑ He was an explorer.
- ⓒ He made a voyage around the world.
- ⓓ He was a favorite of Elizabeth I.
- ⓔ He attempted to start a colony on Roanoke.

13. William and Mary promised to keep the laws made by _____.
    ⓐ previous kings
    ⓑ the pope
    ⓒ Parliament
    ⓓ the Stuarts

14. What event in English history shows us that Parliament believed it should have more power than the king?
    ⓐ the defeat of the Spanish Armada
    ⓑ the crowning of Charles II
    ⓒ the colonization of Roanoke
    ⓓ the Glorious Revolution

15. Which dynasty came after the Tudors in England?
    ⓐ the Stuarts
    ⓑ the Windsors
    ⓒ the Smiths
    ⓓ the Hanovers

Student Guide
Lesson 1: The First Americans

- Recognize that different cultures inhabited North America before the arrival of the Europeans.
- List the Pacific Northwest, desert, Plains, and Eastern woodland peoples as major cultures and describe some of their skills and abilities.
- Describe various motivations of the English who came to the New World (gold, religious freedom, land, freedom from imprisonment).
- Explain that many different kinds of people came to the British colonies in North America.
- Identify key figures and events in early settlement, such as John Smith and the Jamestown settlement, Pilgrims, Puritans, William Penn, and James Oglethorpe.

When the English and French claimed parts of North America, they were coming to a land already inhabited. The first Americans had crossed the land bridge from Asia during the Ice Age. The Pacific Northwest and the Plains were among the places where Native Americans made their homes at the time of European discovery.

Lesson Objectives

- Recognize that different cultures inhabited North America before the arrival of Europeans.
- List the Pacific Northwest, desert, Plains, and Eastern woodland peoples as major cultures and describe some of their skills and abilities.
- Describe various motivations of the English who came to the New World (gold, religious freedom, land, freedom from imprisonment).
- Explain that many different kinds of people came to the British colonies in North America.
- Identify key figures and events in early settlement, such as John Smith and the Jamestown settlement, Pilgrims, Puritans, William Penn, and James Oglethorpe.
- Explain that the first Americans crossed a land bridge to travel from Asia to North America.
- State that native people in the Pacific Northwest were skilled at fishing and whaling.
- Describe southwestern (Pueblo) Indians as desert dwellers.
- Name one crop cultivated by the Pueblo Indians.

PREPARE

Approximate lesson time is 60 minutes.

Materials

For the Student

    📖 Map of North American Indians

    map, world

    History Record Book

    Kids Discover magazine, America 1492

    glue, children's white

    index cards (6)

    pencils, colored 12

    scissors

Optional
        Anasazi by Leonard Everett Fisher

Keywords and Pronunciation
Hopi (HOH-pee)
Makah (muh-KAW)
Pueblo (PWEH-bloh)

LEARN
Activity 1: Sea People and Desert Dwellers (Offline)
Instructions
Get Ready

Whom did Queen Elizabeth ask to organize the first expeditions to America for England? [1]

Which coast of North America did the English explore? [2]

Now let's look at the continent of North America on our map and review some geography. Which ocean is on the east coast of North America? [3]

Which ocean lies off the west coast of North America? [4]

There are at least three great geographic features that divide North America. In the west, a huge mountain chain stretches north to south. What is that mountain range called? [5] Let's label it on your map.

In the center of the map is a very long river with a very long name. What is that river called? [6] Label it on the map.

To the east runs a long mountain chain where (and this is a hint) Johnny Appleseed planted apple trees. What is that range called? [7] Label it on the map--and watch your spelling!

When the English came to North America, they found that they were not alone. Many native peoples lived on this huge continent. How they lived depended on their location. If they lived on the Pacific coast, they used the waters of that great ocean to fish and hunt. If they lived between the Mississippi and the Rockies, they used the flat grassy plains. In these next two lessons, we'll learn how the first Americans got here. We'll also learn about some of the native peoples who were in North America when the English arrived.

In the 1500s the Spanish and Portuguese began to colonize Mexico, Central America, and South America. When they arrived, they found amazing civilizations there. The Aztecs and the Incas were skilled builders of cities, roads, and bridges. These people had created huge empires.

When the English started to explore North America under Elizabeth and then James I, they found native peoples in North America as well. The North Americans were very different from the city-builders to the south. Some were seafarers. Others were desert dwellers. Some hunted buffalo on the plains. Still others lived in forest villages.

Use your map to color the Pacific Northwest region purple. Color the Southwest region red. We'll be learning about native people from these two regions today.

Read *Kids Discover: America 1492*, pages 2 through 7.

Suggested Discussion Questions
Pages 2-3:
  • How do scientists believe the first Americans came from Asia to America? [1]
  • Why did the first Americans cross the land bridge from Asia to North America? [2]
  • What kinds of large animals did they hope to hunt? [3]
Pages 4-5:

184

- Where were the Makah (muh-KAW) located? [4]
- What kinds of animals did the Makah and other northwestern Indians hunt? [5]
- What kind of boat did the Makah use to catch whales? [6]
- What is a potlatch? [7]

Pages 6-7:

- What kind of climate did southwestern Indians have? [8]
- What were their homes made of? [9]
- What were the Hopi (HOH-pee) especially good at preserving? [10]
- Why did the Hopi need to preserve water? [11]
- What kinds of crops did they grow? [12]

The first Americans were Ice Age hunters who crossed the land bridge in search of caribou, woolly mammoth, and other large animals. They kept moving south. Over time they settled along the northwest coast in lands washed by the Pacific. Salmon and halibut, seal and whales became important to the Makah and many others in this ocean region.

Further south and to the east, water was not nearly as plentiful. Desert dwellers in the Southwest made the best of what they had. These Pueblo (PWEH-bloh) Indians built homes of stone and clay, and grew hearty corn in a land that always seemed to cry out, "Water!"

Show You Know

How do historians believe the first Americans traveled to North America? [1]

What were the northwestern Indians skilled at hunting? [2]

In what kind of region did southwestern Indians dwell, desert or forest? [3]

Name a crop the southwestern Indians were able to grow in this region. [4]

Activity 2: History Record Book (Offline)
Instructions

Choose either A or B.

A. Written Narration Write two to four sentences explaining what the lesson was about. If necessary, use the Show You Know questions to help get started. Only include the most important parts of the lesson. Write your name, the date, and the lesson title on your written narration, and put it in your History Record Book.

Sample written narration: "The first Americans came across a giant land bridge from Asia. Some of them hunted in canoes for seals and whales. The Indians in the desert needed to save all the water they could. They grew crops like corn and beans."

B. Picture Narration Draw a picture of the part of the lesson that interested you most. When you have finished drawing, describe the picture. Below your picture, write a description of what you have drawn. Write your name, the date, and the lesson title on your picture narration, and put it in your History Record Book.

Activity 3: Native Americans of North America, Part 1 *(Offline)*
Instructions
Follow these directions to make a presentation map of the first Americans.

1. Draw an outline map of North America. Include the eastern tip of Asia (present-day Siberia). Use the map of North America on page 3 of *Kids Discover: America 1492* as a reference. For now, leave the entire continent white. Label the Arctic Ocean, Pacific Ocean, Atlantic Ocean, North America, and Asia. Add a title at the top of the map: "Native Americans of North America."

2. Cut arrows out of construction paper and glue them to the map to show the movement of the people who crossed the land bridge from Asia to North America. Show the route from Asia to present-day Alaska, Canada, the Pacific Northwest, and the American Southwest.

3. Select one of the following topics from page 2: the first Americans, the ground sloth, spear points, or the wooly mammoth. Write three to five sentences about the topic on an index card. Include a drawing if you wish. Attach the index card to the map near present-day Alaska.

4. On another index card, write a short paragraph about the Makah. Reread pages 4 and 5 if you need to refresh your memory. Attach this index card to the map near present-day Washington state. Show where the Makah lived by shading the region a color of your choice.

5. Draw one of the following on an index card, label it, and attach it to the map: canoe, harpoon, cedar basket, or canoe paddle. (See pages 4 and 5.)

6. On an index card, write a short paragraph about the Hopi. Reread pages 6 and 7 if necessary. Attach the index card to the map near the present-day southwestern United States (northeastern Arizona). Show where the Hopi lived by shading the region a different color from the one you used for the Makah.

7. Draw one of the following on an index card, label it, and attach it to the map: corn, kachina doll, or pueblo (Hopi dwelling). (See pages 6 and 7.)

You will finish this project in the People of the Plains and Forest lesson.

ASSESS

Lesson Assessment: The First Americans (*Online*)
You will complete an offline assessment covering the main objectives of this lesson. Your learning coach will score this assessment.

LEARN

Activity 4. Optional: The First Americans *(Offline)*
Instructions
Check your library or bookstore for *Anasazi*, by Leonard Everett Fisher (New York: Atheneum, 1997). This fascinating book is illustrated with acrylic paintings done in moody sepia tones. From what little is known of these mysterious people, the author puts together a picture of Anasazi life.

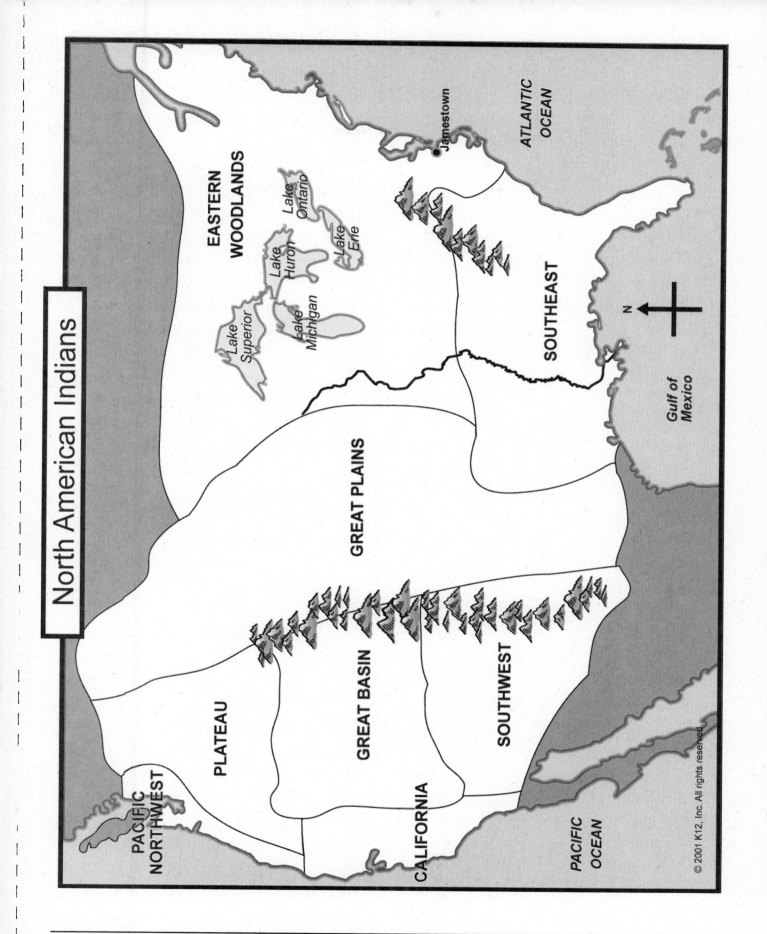

North American Indians

EASTERN WOODLANDS

Lake Superior
Lake Michigan
Lake Huron
Lake Erie
Lake Ontario

Jamestown

ATLANTIC OCEAN

SOUTHEAST

Gulf of Mexico

N

GREAT PLAINS

PLATEAU

GREAT BASIN

SOUTHWEST

PACIFIC NORTHWEST

CALIFORNIA

PACIFIC OCEAN

Lesson Assessment

The First Americans

1. How do historians believe the first Americans traveled to North

   America?_____

2. What were the northwestern Indians skilled at hunting?_____

3. In what kind of region did southwestern Indians dwell, desert or forest?_____

4. Name a crop the southwestern Indians were able to grow in this region._____

Student Guide
Lesson 2: People of the Plains and Forest

East of the Rocky Mountains and west of the Mississippi River lay broad plains covered with grass. The Great Plains were home to the buffalo and to the native peoples who lived by hunting them. In the forests east of the Mississippi, woodland tribes hunted deer, fished streams, and planted "the three sisters": beans, squash, and corn.

Lesson Objectives

- Locate the Rocky Mountains, Great Plains, Mississippi River, and Appalachians on a map.
- Explain that the Plains Indians hunted buffalo for food and clothing.
- Describe Eastern Woodland tribes as forest dwellers who hunted and farmed.
- Name one Plains tribe and one Eastern Woodland tribe.

PREPARE

Approximate lesson time is 60 minutes.

Materials

For the Student

    📖 Map of North American Indians

    History Record Book

    Kids Discover magazine, America 1492

    crayons 8

    glue, children's white

    household items - clay, blue yarn

    index cards (6)

    previous lesson material - unfinished map

Keywords and Pronunciation
Iroquois (IR-uh-kwoy)
Mandan (MAN-dan)

LEARN
Activity 1: Farmers, Hunters, and Town Builders *(Offline)*
Instructions
Get Ready

Which group of Native American people used the waters of the Pacific for their livelihood? [1]
What did they like to hunt? [2]
What kind of land did the the Indians of the Southwest live on? [3]
What did they build their homes with? [4]

Native people of the Pacific Northwest and the American Southwest lived on the western side of the large mountain range called the Rockies. Today we'll move east and learn about two large Native American groups that lived east of the Rockies.

The first people we'll study are perhaps the most famous of all Native Americans, the Great Plains tribes. The Great Plains are wide, flat grasslands flanked by the giant Rocky Mountains in the west and the long Mississippi River in the east. The buffalo loved these grasslands, and early Americans did, too.

On your map, color the Great Plains yellow.

After we learn about the Plains Indians, we'll head east of the Mississippi and learn about the Eastern Woodland tribes. East of the Mississippi, a region of forest stretched all the way to the Atlantic Ocean. The Appalachian Mountains rose like a giant spine through the forest. Eastern Woodland tribes were at home in this area of wooded hills.

On your map, color the Eastern Woodlands region green.

Read *Kids Discover: America 1492,* pages 8 through 15.

Suggested Discussion Questions

Pages 8-9:

- How would you describe the Great Plains? [1]
- How did the Plains Indians catch buffalo? [2]
- How did the Mandan (MAN-dan) people use the buffalo? [3]
- What other animal helped with the buffalo hunt? [4]

Pages 10-11 (after looking at the animal chart):

What other parts of North America had buffalo in 1492? [5]

Pages 12-13:

- How would you describe the eastern half of north America in 1492? [6]
- Who were the Iroquois (IR-uh-kwoy)? [7]
- What animals did they hunt? [8]
- What were boys trained to be? [9]
- Who did most of the farming? [10]
- What kind of homes did the Iroquois have? [11]
- What game did the Iroquois invent? [12]

Pages 14-15:

- Who were the Creek Indians? [13]
- Why were they called Creeks? [14]
- How did they hunt deer? [15]
- What were the three crops that women planted? [16]

The Plains and Eastern Woodland peoples lived in the ways nature made possible in their different regions. Indians west of the Mississippi hunted the plentiful buffalo and lived on the grassy plains. Indians east of the Mississippi made a home in the forest, where deer, moose, and bears provided food and clothing.

None of the North American tribes that the English would meet built large cities like their neighbors to the south. No emperor reigned over them all. The peoples were many and their lives were varied. They were people of the ocean, desert, plains and forests. They were seafarers, hunters, farmers, and sometimes warriors. In the next lesson, we'll find out what happened when members of those Eastern Woodland tribes met colonists from England.

Show You Know

Find the Rocky Mountains, Great Plains, Mississippi River, and Appalachians on the map.

What animal was especially important to the Plains Indians? [1]

Why did the Plains Indians hunt buffalo? [2]

What kind of land did eastern Indian tribes live in? [3]

How did they make their living? [4]

What is the name of one Plains tribe? [5]

What is the name of one Eastern Woodland tribe? [6]

Activity 2: History Record Book (Offline)
Instructions

Choose either A or B.

A. Written Narration: Write two to four sentences explaining what the lesson was about. If necessary, use the Show You Know questions to help get started. Only include the most important parts of the lesson. Write your name, the date, and the lesson title on your written narration, and put it in your History Record Book.

Sample written narration: "Native Americans lived in different places and lived in different ways. The Plains Indians hunted buffalo. The Eastern Woodland tribes lived in the forest. They hunted animals like deer and grew food like squash and beans."

B. Picture Narration: Draw a picture of the part of the lesson that interested you most. When you have finished drawing, describe the picture. Below your picture, write a description of what you have drawn. Write your name, the date, and the lesson title on your picture narration, and put it in your History Record Book.

Activity 3: Native Americans of North America, Part 2 (Offline)
Instructions

Complete the project you started in the First Americans lesson by following these directions. The page numbers refer to *Kids Discover: America 1492.*

1. Select one of the following topics from pages 8 and 9: Mandan earth lodges or hunting buffalo. Write three to five sentences about the topic on an index card. Include a drawing if you wish. Attach the index card to the map near present-day North Dakota.

2. On another index card, write a short paragraph about the Mandan. Reread pages 8 and 9 if you need to refresh your memory. Attach the index card to the map near present-day North Dakota. Show where the Mandan lived by shading the region another color.

3. Select one of the following topics from pages 12 and 13: Iroquois longhouses, lacrosse, or Iroquois crops. Write three to five sentences about the topic on an index card. Include a drawing if you wish. Attach the index card to the map near present-day New York State.

4. On an index card, write a paragraph about the Iroquois. Reread pages 12 and 13 if necessary. Attach the card to the map near present-day New York State. Show where the Iroquois lived by shading the region another color.

5. Select one of the following topics from pages 14 and 15: the Green Corn ceremony, hunting, or the temple mound. Write three to five sentences about the topic on an index card. Include a drawing if you wish. Attach the index card to the map near present-day South Carolina.

6. On an index card, write a paragraph about the Creek. Reread pages 14 and 15 if necessary. Attach the card to the map near present-day South Carolina. Show where the Creek lived by shading the region another color.

7. Use clay and blue yarn to show where the Rocky and Appalachian Mountains and the Mississippi River are located. Think of something that would represent the Great Plains and place it on the map to show this region's location. Label these geographic features. Now you are ready to display your map of Native Americans of North America.

ASSESS

Lesson Assessment: People of the Plains and Forest (*Online*)

You will complete an offline assessment covering the main objectives of this lesson. Your learning coach will score this assessment.

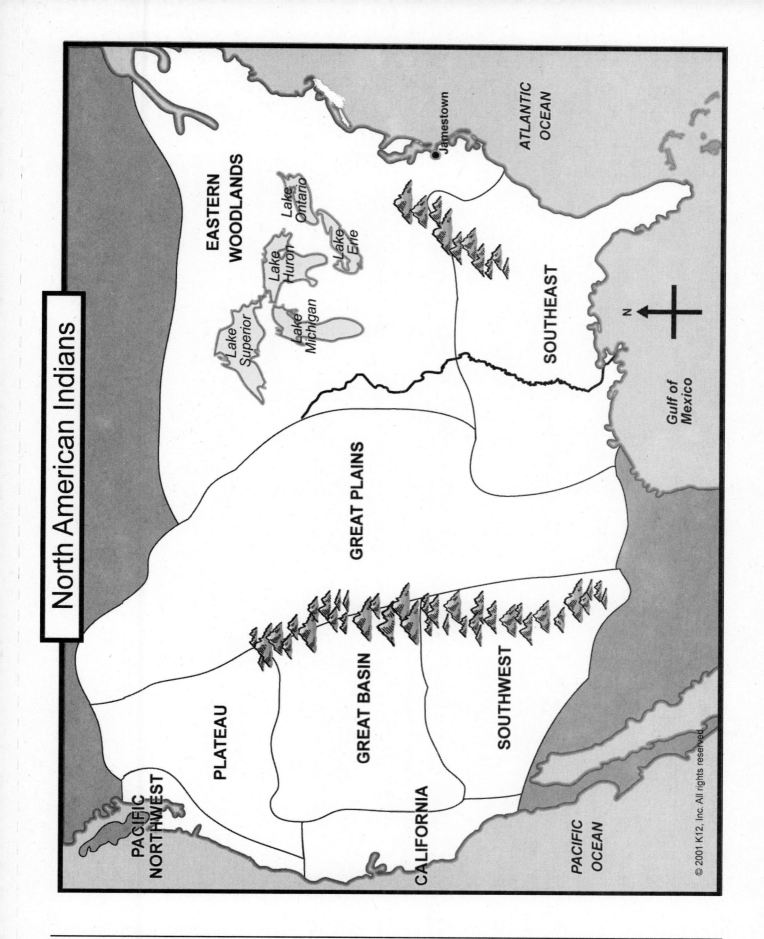

North American Indians

EASTERN WOODLANDS

Lake Superior
Lake Michigan
Lake Huron
Lake Ontario
Lake Erie

Jamestown

ATLANTIC OCEAN

SOUTHEAST

Gulf of Mexico

N

GREAT PLAINS

PLATEAU

GREAT BASIN

SOUTHWEST

PACIFIC NORTHWEST

CALIFORNIA

PACIFIC OCEAN

© 2001 K12, Inc. All rights reserved.

Lesson Assessment Key

People of the Plains and Forest

1. **In order to answer this question, use the map of North American Indians.**
   Where are the Rocky Mountains, Great Plains, Mississippi River, and Appalachian Mountains located?

2. Why did the Plains Indians hunt buffalo?_____

3. What kind of land did eastern Indian tribes live in?_____

4. What is the name of one Plains tribe?_____

5. What is the name of one Eastern Woodland tribe?_____

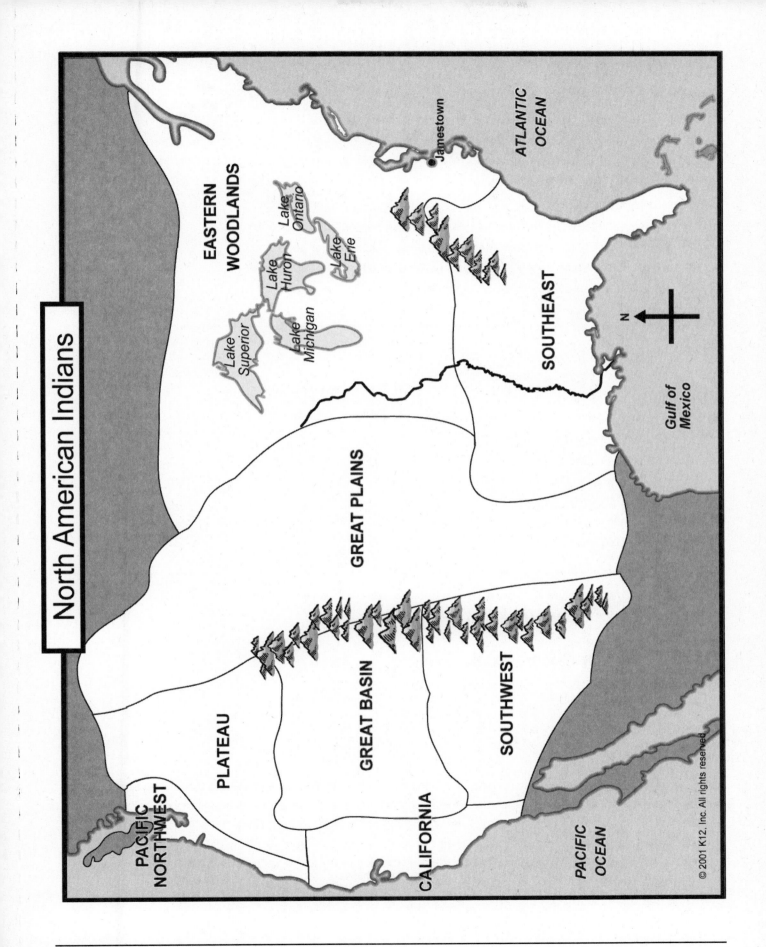

North American Indians

EASTERN WOODLANDS

Lake Ontario
Lake Erie
Lake Huron
Lake Michigan
Lake Superior

Jamestown

ATLANTIC OCEAN

SOUTHEAST

Gulf of Mexico

N

GREAT PLAINS

PLATEAU

GREAT BASIN

SOUTHWEST

PACIFIC NORTHWEST

CALIFORNIA

PACIFIC OCEAN

Student Guide
Lesson 3: The Story of Jamestown

Eager not to be left behind in the European race for New World treasures, the English established their first permanent colony at Jamestown. The tough leader of the colony, John Smith, taught the colonists that gold was not nearly as important as survival.

Lesson Objectives

- Name Jamestown as the first successful English settlement in North America.
- Explain that the English started the Jamestown colony to find gold.
- Identify John Smith as the leader who saved Jamestown.
- Describe the hard experience at Jamestown.

PREPARE

Approximate lesson time is 60 minutes.

Materials

For the Student

    📖 Map of Early American Settlements

    History Record Book

    📖 Jamestown Diary activity sheet

Keywords and Pronunciation

colony : A land ruled by a faraway country.

Powhatan (pow-uh-TAN)

LEARN
Activity 1: Colonies in Virginia *(Online)*

Activity 2: History Record Book *(Offline)*
Instructions

Choose either A or B.

A. Written Narration

Write two to four sentences explaining what the lesson was about. If necessary, use the Show You Know questions to help get started. Only include the most important parts of the lesson. Write your name, the date, and the lesson title on your written narration, and put it in your History Record Book.

Sample written narration: "The settlers at Jamestown came looking for gold, but they did not find any. Many of them were not used to working. John Smith made them work harder. Many settlers died, but finally Jamestown started to grow."

B. Picture Narration

Draw a picture of the part of the lesson that interested you most. When you have finished drawing, describe the picture. Below your picture, write a description of what you have drawn. Write your name, the date, and the lesson title on your picture narration, and put it in your History Record Book.

Activity 3: Jamestown Diary (Offline)
Instructions
Much of what we know about Jamestown and other early settlements in the New World comes from diaries and journals. Make your own Jamestown diary using the Jamestown Diary activity sheet.

1. Cut out each of the four pages.
2. Write your entry for each page.
3. Cut out two pieces of brown construction paper that are slightly larger than the diary pages. These will be the front and back covers of the diary.
4. Punch holes where shown on the diary pages and in the appropriate locations on the covers.
5. Use pieces of yarn to bind the pages between the covers.

If you're having trouble deciding what to write for each entry, reread the following sections of Jamestown's Rocky Start in the Reading Room:
- 1607: page 2, paragraphs 2 and 3
- 1608: page 4, paragraphs 1 and 2
- 1609: page 4, last paragraph
- 1610: page 6, first paragraph

ASSESS
Lesson Assessment: The Story of Jamestown (Online)
You will complete an offline assessment covering the main objectives of this lesson. Your learning coach will score this assessment.

LEARN
Activity 4. Optional: The Story of Jamestown (Online)
Learn more about Jamestown on the Web.

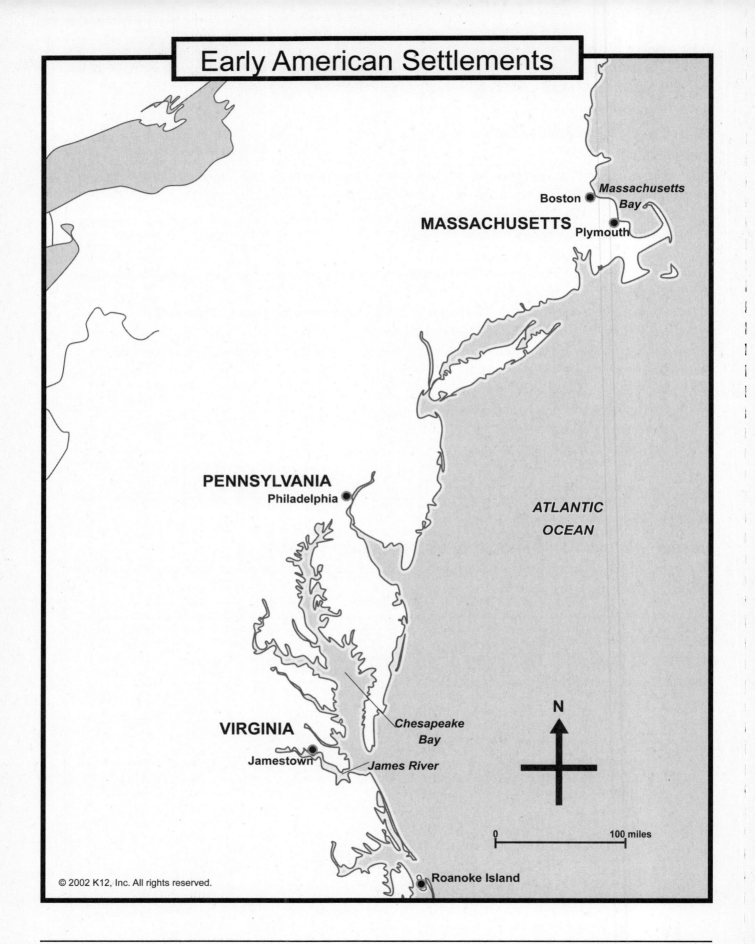

Early American Settlements

MASSACHUSETTS

Boston ● *Massachusetts Bay*

Plymouth ●

PENNSYLVANIA

Philadelphia ●

ATLANTIC OCEAN

Chesapeake Bay

VIRGINIA

Jamestown ●

James River

N

0   100 miles

Roanoke Island ●

Jamestown Diary

Each entry in the diary contains an actual quote from a Jamestown settler. Write two to four sentences that help to further describe what was going on during this time.

September 10, 1608

"... the Church was repaired; the Store-house recovered; buildings prepared for the Supplyes, we expected; ... the squadrons trained ..."

John Smith was elected president of the council.

May 13, 1607

"The thirteenth day, we came to our seating place ... where our shippes doe lie so neere the shoare that they are moored to the Trees ..."

We left England on the 20th and sailed across the Atlantic.

May 23, 1610

"Viewing the fort, we found the palisades torn down, the ports open, the gates from off the hinges, and the empty houses rent up and burnt . . ."

Two ships arrived from England bringing

fresh supplies.

August 1609

". . . in 3 monthes we made . . . sope ashes . . . made a well in the forte of excellent sweete water . . . 30 or 40 acres of ground we digged, and planted . . ."

Seven ships arrived from England bringing

men, women, and children.

Name _____ Date _____

Lesson Assessment

The Story of Jamestown

1. What was the name of the first successful English settlement in North America? _____

2. What did the colonists at Jamestown hope to find? _____

3. Which brave leader helped Jamestown survive? _____

4. What were some of the difficulties the English had to overcome in

   Jamestown? _____

Student Guide
Lesson 4: The Story of Plymouth Colony

Seeking the freedom to worship as they wished, a small band of Pilgrims sailed from England on the *Mayflower*. Landing far north of their intended destination, the Pilgrims founded Plymouth Colony in what is now Massachusetts. They survived a dreadful first winter and celebrated a bountiful harvest--all with the help of the Indians.

Lesson Objectives

- Describe Plymouth as a colony begun for religious freedom.
- Name the *Mayflower* as the boat on which the Pilgrims sailed.
- Recognize the key role of the Indians in assisting the Pilgrims through their first year.
- Describe Thanksgiving as the festival in which the Pilgrims thanked God for their harvest.

PREPARE

Approximate lesson time is 60 minutes.

Materials

For the Student

- Map of Early American Settlements
  History Record Book
- Pilgrim Story activity sheet
  glue, children's white
  paper, construction - assorted colors
  pencils, colored 12
  scissors

Keywords and Pronunciation

Samoset (SAM-uh-set)
Squanto (SKWAHN-toh)

LEARN
Activity 1: A Landing in Massachusetts *(Online)*

Activity 2: History Record Book *(Offline)*

Instructions

Choose either A or B.

A. Written Narration Write two to four sentences explaining what the lesson was about. If necessary, use the Show You Know questions to help get started. Only include the most important parts of the lesson. Write your name, the date, and the lesson title on your written narration, and put it in your History Record Book.

Sample written narration: "The Pilgrims left England so they could worship God they way they wanted. They sailed on the Mayflower and came to Plymouth. Their first winter was very hard, but the Indians helped them get food. They held a feast to thank God for the harvest."

B. Picture Narration Draw a picture of the part of the lesson that interested you most. When you have finished drawing, describe the picture. Below your picture, write a description of what you have drawn. Write your name, the date, and the lesson title on your picture narration, and put it in your History Record Book.

Activity 3: Turkey Tells the Pilgrim Story *(Offline)*

Instructions

Print out the activity sheet and follow these directions to make a turkey whose feathers tell the story of the Pilgrims.

1. Write two to four sentences on each feather on pages 2 and 3 to complete the paragraph.

2. Cut out the feathers, glue them to pieces of construction paper, and cut the construction paper around the feathers, leaving a border.

3. Cut out the patterns on pages 4 and 5 and use them to trace the turkey's body, head, and foot on construction paper.

4. Cut out the turkey's body, head, and foot from the construction paper and decorate them as you like.

5. Glue the turkey together as shown on page 1 of the activity sheet.

ASSESS

Lesson Assessment: The Story of Plymouth Colony (*Online*)

You will complete an offline assessment covering the main objectives of this lesson. Your learning coach will score this assessment.

LEARN

Activity 4. Optional: The Story of Plymouth Colony *(Online)*

Learn about the *Mayflower* by taking a look at the *Mayflower II.*

Turkey Tells the Pilgrim Story

Follow these directions to make a turkey whose feathers tell the story of the Pilgrims.

1. Write two to four sentences on each feather on pages 2 and 3 to complete the paragraph.

2. Cut out the feathers, glue them to pieces of construction paper, and cut the construction paper around the feathers, leaving a border.

3. Cut out the patterns on pages 4 and 5 and use them to trace the turkey's body, head, and foot on construction paper.

4. Cut out the turkey's body, head, and foot from the construction paper and decorate them as you like.

5. Glue the turkey together as shown below.

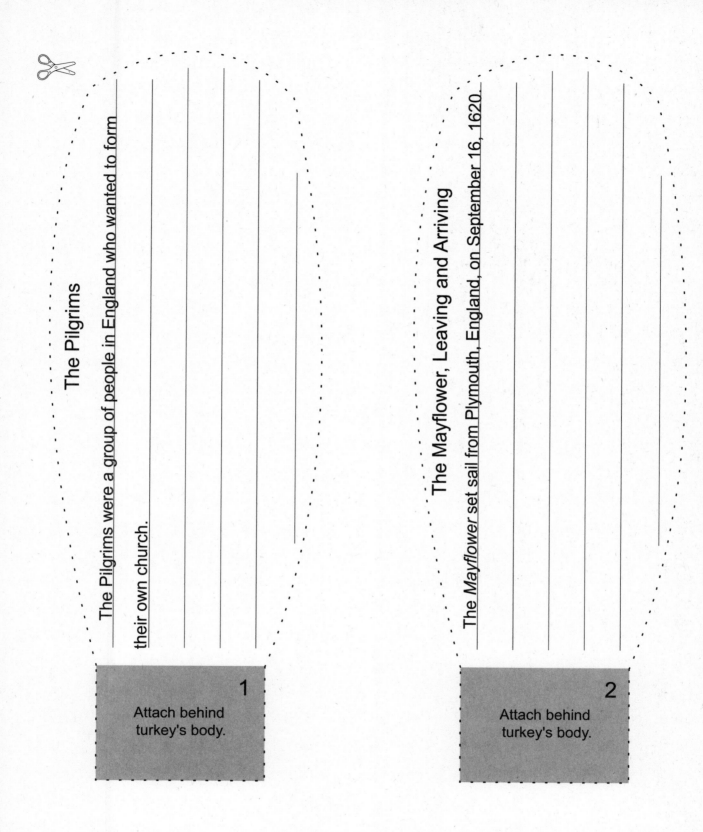

The Pilgrims

The Pilgrims were a group of people in England who wanted to form their own church.

1
Attach behind turkey's body.

The Mayflower, Leaving and Arriving

The *Mayflower* set sail from Plymouth, England, on September 16, 1620.

2
Attach behind turkey's body.

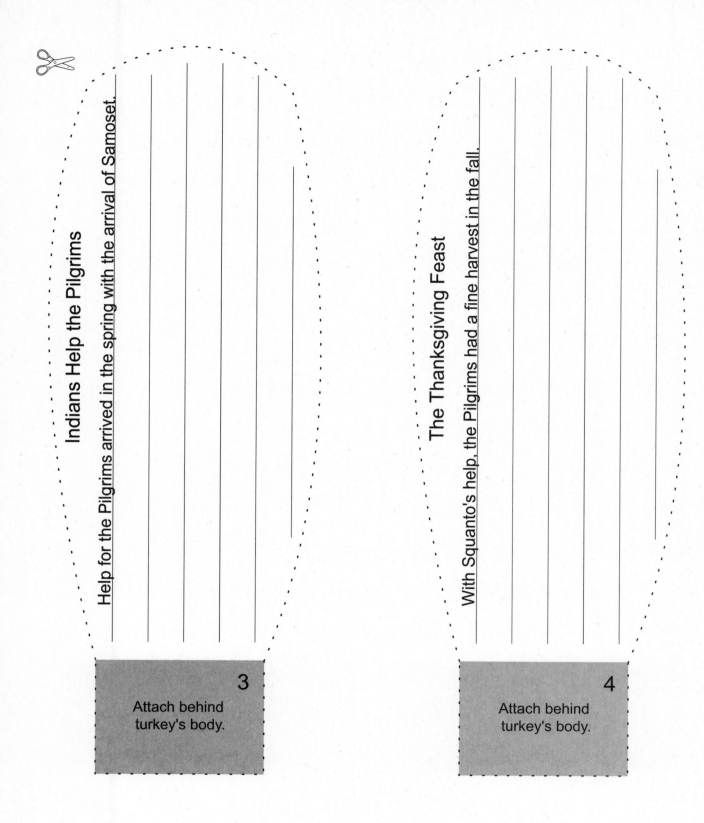

Indians Help the Pilgrims

Help for the Pilgrims arrived in the spring with the arrival of Samoset.

3

Attach behind turkey's body.

The Thanksgiving Feast

With Squanto's help, the Pilgrims had a fine harvest in the fall.

4

Attach behind turkey's body.

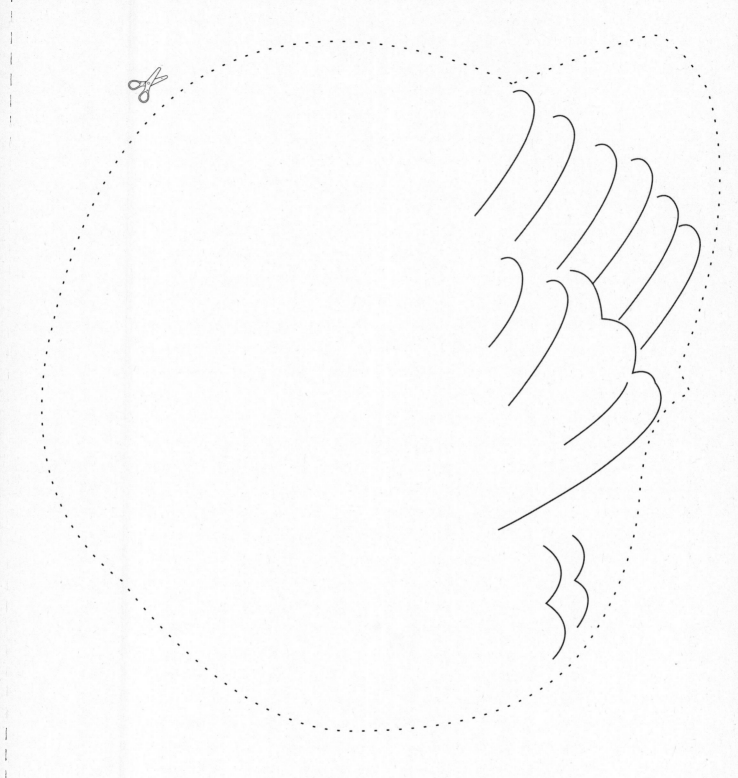

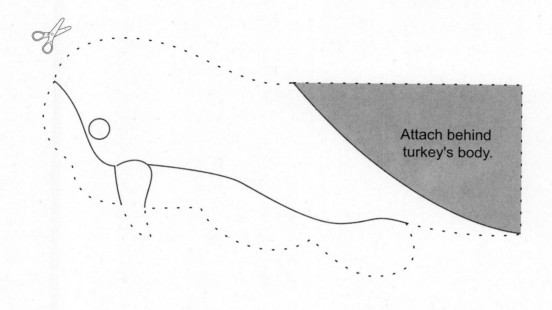

Attach behind turkey's body.

Attach behind turkey's body.

Early American Settlements

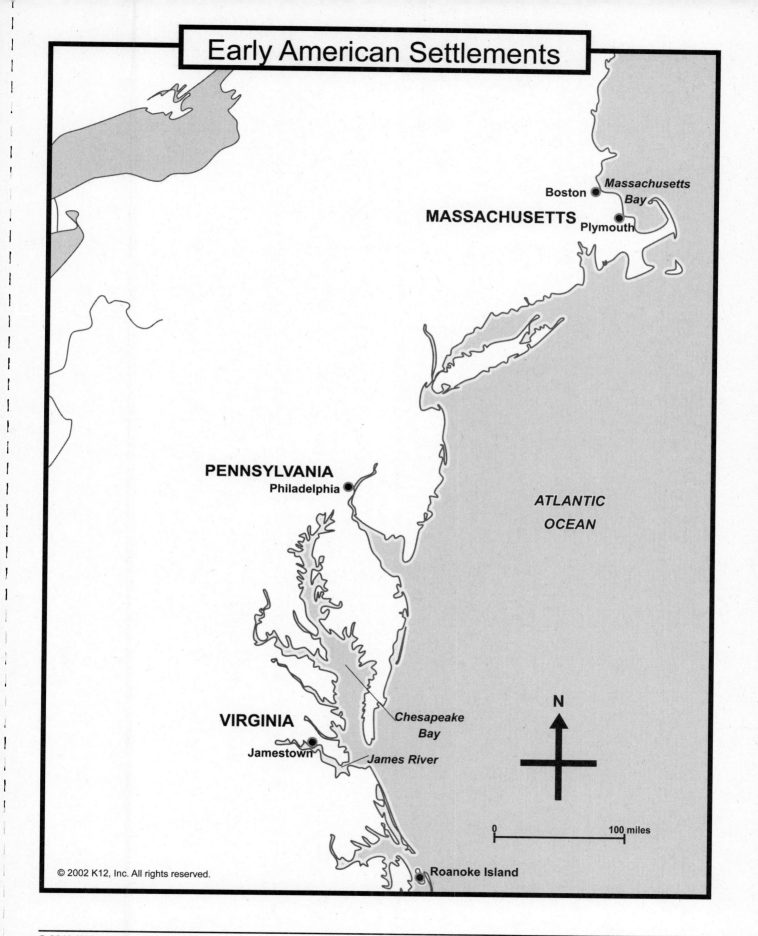

Boston

Massachusetts Bay

MASSACHUSETTS

Plymouth

PENNSYLVANIA

Philadelphia

ATLANTIC OCEAN

VIRGINIA

Jamestown

Chesapeake Bay

James River

N

0   100 miles

Roanoke Island

Lesson Assessment

The Story of Plymouth Colony

1. Why did the Pilgrims leave England and start a colony in America? _____

2. What was the name of the ship on which they sailed? _____

3. Who helped the Pilgrims in the spring? _____

4. How did the Indians help? _____

5. What was Thanksgiving? _____

Student Guide
Lesson 5: The Story of William Penn

William Penn, a well-educated Quaker trained in the law, started the mid Atlantic colony of Pennsylvania. He wanted it to be a place of refuge for Quakers and people of all faiths.

Lesson Objectives

- Name the Puritans as another group that came to America for religious freedom.
- Describe William Penn as the founder of Pennsylvania.
- Explain that Pennsylvania was founded for religious freedom for Quakers and others.
- State that *Philadelphia* means "City of Brotherly Love."

PREPARE

Approximate lesson time is 60 minutes.

Materials

For the Student

    🖥 Map of Early American Settlements

    History Record Book

    🖥 England Begins to Colonize activity sheet

Keywords and Pronunciation

English Parliament (PAHR-luh-muhnt) : The lawmaking body of England, including representatives of the nobility and of the commoners.

LEARN
Activity 1: In Search of Religious Freedom (Online)

Activity 2: History Record Book (Offline)
Instructions

Choose either A or B.

A. Written Narration

Write two to four sentences explaining what the lesson was about. If necessary, use the Show You Know questions to help get started. Only include the most important parts of the lesson. Write your name, the date, and the lesson title on your written narration, and put it in your History Record Book.

Sample written narration: "William Penn was a Quaker. He wanted to have a place in America where people of all religions could live in peace. The king gave him land for Pennsylvania. He started a city there called Philadelphia, which means City of Brotherly Love."

B. Picture Narration

Draw a picture of the part of the lesson that interested you most. When you have finished drawing, describe the picture. Below your picture, write a description of what you have drawn. Write your name, the date, and the lesson title on your picture narration, and put it in your History Record Book.

Activity 3: England Begins to Colonize (Offline)
Instructions
Complete the England Begins to Colonize activity sheet to review information about the four English colonies in North America that you've studied.

ASSESS
Lesson Assessment: The Story of William Penn (Online)
You will complete an offline assessment covering the main objectives of this lesson. Your learning coach will score this assessment.

LEARN
Activity 4. Optional: The Story of William Penn (Offline)
Instructions
Use two or more different types of resources to learn more about Philadelphia. Read about the Liberty Bell and Independence Hall. Choose one of these to describe in a paragraph. Draw a picture of the one you wrote about.

Name _____   Date _____

England Begins to Colonize

In the boxes, write the names of the four English colonies given below, in the order in which they were founded. Then fill in the blanks below the time line.

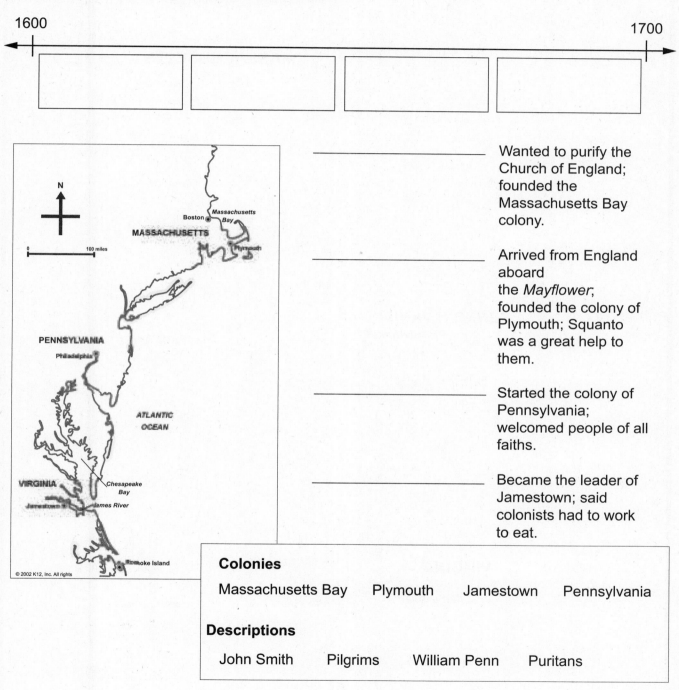

1600   1700

_____ Wanted to purify the Church of England; founded the Massachusetts Bay colony.

_____ Arrived from England aboard the *Mayflower*; founded the colony of Plymouth; Squanto was a great help to them.

_____ Started the colony of Pennsylvania; welcomed people of all faiths.

_____ Became the leader of Jamestown; said colonists had to work to eat.

Colonies

Massachusetts Bay   Plymouth   Jamestown   Pennsylvania

Descriptions

John Smith   Pilgrims   William Penn   Puritans

Early American Settlements

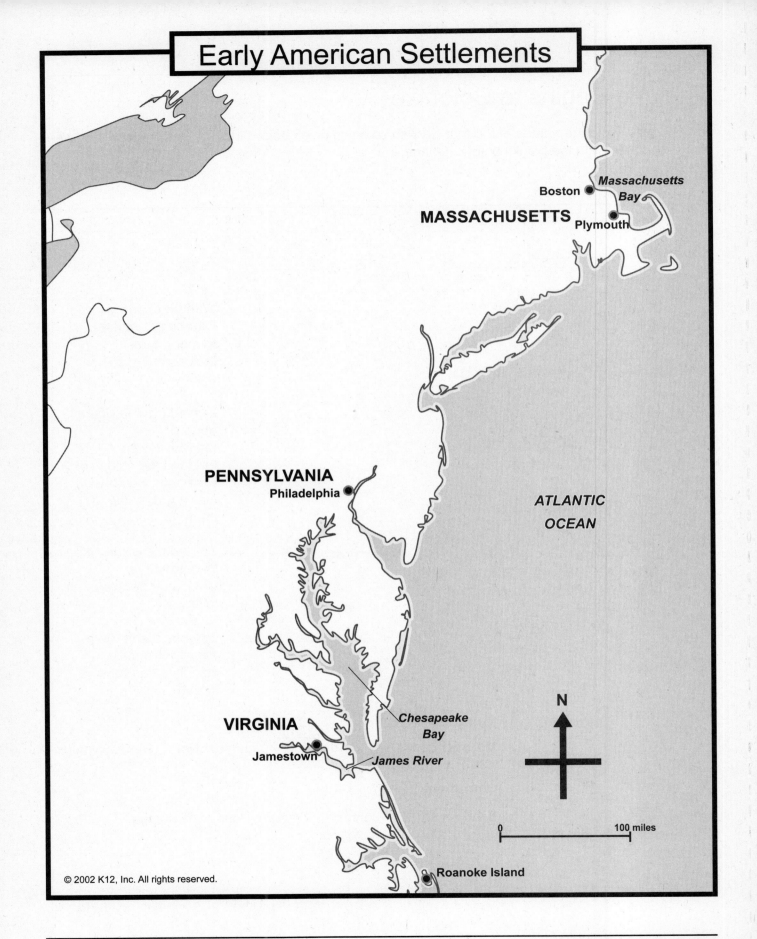

Boston ●
Massachusetts Bay
MASSACHUSETTS
Plymouth ●

PENNSYLVANIA
Philadelphia ●

ATLANTIC OCEAN

Chesapeake Bay

VIRGINIA
Jamestown ●
James River

N

0   100 miles

Roanoke Island ●

Name _____ Date _____

Lesson Assessment

The Story of William Penn

1. Which group of English colonists lived near the Pilgrims and founded the colony of Massachusetts

   Bay?_____

2. Who started a Quaker colony in America?_____

3. Why did William Penn start a colony?_____

4. What does Philadelphia mean?_____

Student Guide
Lesson 6: More Colonists in Maryland and Georgia

English colonists founded Maryland as a haven for Catholics and Georgia as a refuge for debtors. Georgia was the last of the 13 English colonies in North America.

Lesson Objectives

- State that Maryland was founded for religious freedom for Catholics.
- Explain that Georgia was founded as a refuge for debtors.
- State that by the 1730s there were 13 English colonies on the east coast of North America.

PREPARE

Approximate lesson time is 60 minutes.

Materials

For the Student

- Map of The Thirteen Colonies, 1763
- History Record Book
- Colonists Wanted activity sheet

Keywords and Pronunciation

debtor : A person who owes another person money.

James Oglethorpe (OH-guhl-thorp)

LEARN
Activity 1: The Maryland and Georgia Colonies (Online)

Activity 2: History Record Book (Offline)
Instructions

Choose either A or B.

A. Written Narration

Write two to four sentences explaining what the lesson was about. If necessary, use the Show You Know questions to help get started. Only include the most important parts of the lesson. Write your name, the date, and the lesson title on your written narration, and put it in your History Record Book.

Sample written narration: "George Calvert founded Maryland to be a place where Catholics could worship. James Oglethorpe decided to start Georgia. It was a colony for debtors. There were 13 English colonies in all."

B. Picture Narration

Draw a picture of the part of the lesson that interested you most. When you have finished drawing, describe the picture. Below your picture, write a description of what you have drawn. Write your name, the date, and the lesson title on your picture narration, and put it in your History Record Book.

Activity 3: Settlers Wanted for Maryland and Georgia *(Offline)*

Instructions

In England in 1700 people used handbills to advertise. Handbills were small printed sheets that were given out by hand. Merchants selling goods could have handbills printed and distributed advertising their goods for sale.

Pretend you are in charge of finding people to settle in the new colonies of Maryland and Georgia. Create two handbills: one that advertises for colonists for Maryland, and one for Georgia. Print the Colonists Wanted activity sheet to see an example of a handbill.

When writing your ads, remember the following points:

Maryland

1. Maryland was founded by an English nobleman, George Calvert, who became a Catholic in Protestant England.
2. In England, Catholics were not allowed to practice their religion openly.
3. Calvert had tried to set up a colony earlier in Newfoundland, but it was too cold there.
4. The first colonists arrived in 1634.
5. The soil in Maryland was fertile, there were a lot of trees, and the climate was mild.
6. There was a lot of food to be found in the woods and waters of Maryland.
7. The colony had a successful start with a good first harvest, and even exported surplus corn to Massachusetts.

Georgia

1. Georgia was founded by James Oglethorpe, a wealthy English politican.
2. The colony was founded as a place where debtors could start a new life.
3. Debtors are people who cannot pay their bills.
4. Georgia was named for King George II of England.
5. There were many plans created for the new colony.
6. The climate was hot in the summer.
7. The settlers cut down pine trees and sold the wood to the English navy.
8. They grew rice in Georgia's swampy lowlands.

ASSESS

Lesson Assessment: More Colonists in Maryland and Georgia *(Online)*

You will complete an offline assessment covering the main objectives of this lesson. Your learning coach will score this assessment.

LEARN

Activity 4. Optional: More Colonists in Maryland and Georgia *(Online)*

The Thirteen Colonies, 1763

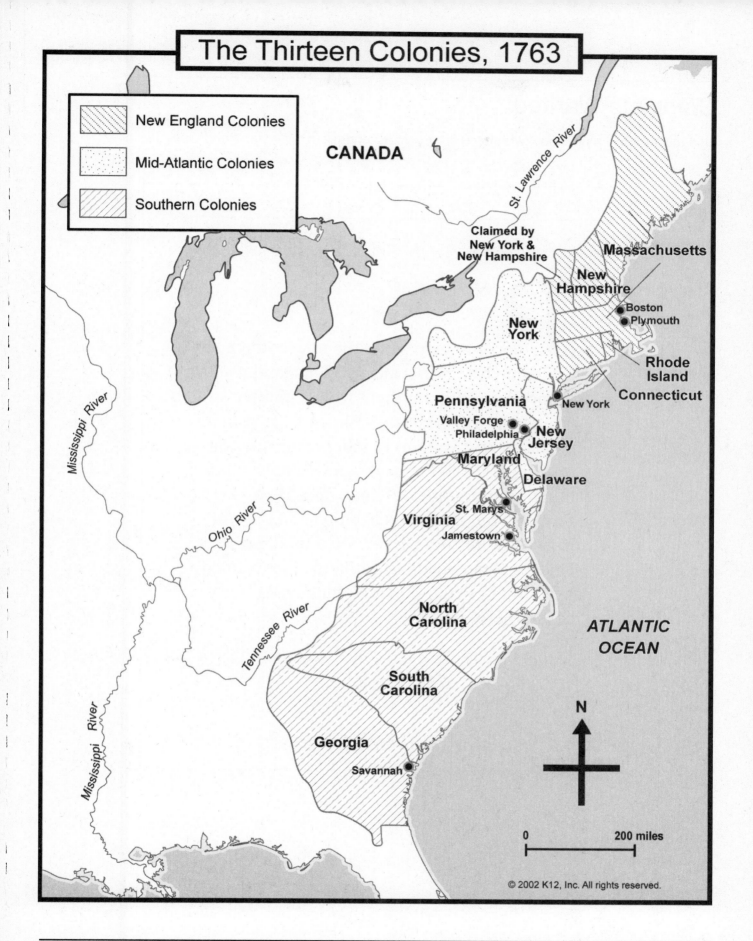

Legend:
- New England Colonies
- Mid-Atlantic Colonies
- Southern Colonies

CANADA

St. Lawrence River

Claimed by New York & New Hampshire

Massachusetts

New Hampshire

Boston
Plymouth

New York

Rhode Island

Connecticut

Pennsylvania

New York

Valley Forge
Philadelphia

New Jersey

Maryland

Delaware

St. Marys

Virginia

Jamestown

Mississippi River

Ohio River

Tennessee River

North Carolina

ATLANTIC OCEAN

South Carolina

Georgia

Savannah

Mississippi River

N

0   200 miles

Name _____ Date _____

Colonists Wanted

Use this handbill as a model when you create your handbills for Maryland and Georgia.

WANTED

People to help settle the new colony of Pennsylvania in America. This land was founded by William Penn from a charter granted by His Majesty Charles II. If you are a Quaker and want to practice your religion openly, come to Pennsylvania. People from other religions are welcome, too. Be a farmer—the climate is healthy, and the soil is rich and fertile. Or are you a merchant? Live in the new city of Philadelphia. Named by William Penn, Philadelphia means "City of Brotherly Love."

Lesson Assessment

More Colonists in Maryland and Georgia

1. Which colony was founded as a place for Catholics to worship freely?_____

2. For what group did James Oglethorpe start Georgia?_____

3. How many English colonies were there on the east coast of North America after Georgia was founded?_____

Student Guide
Lesson 7: From Many Lands

By 1750, there were 13 British colonies along the Atlantic seaboard. Not all the colonists were from England. Germans, Irish, and Dutch settled alongside the English. Africans were brought to the British colonies as well, and African slaves became a large part of the workforce in the plantation South.

Lesson Objectives

- State that New York was originally Dutch.
- Name some other nationalities of the colonists, such as German, Irish, and Dutch.
- Define a plantation as a large farm that required a lot of laborers.
- Explain that African slaves became a large part of the workforce in the South.

PREPARE

Approximate lesson time is 60 minutes.

Materials

For the Student

📖 Map of The Thirteen Colonies, 1763

History Record Book

📖 Mapping the Thirteen Colonies

Keywords and Pronunciation

plantation (plan-TAY-shuhn) : A large farm that is worked by resident laborers.

LEARN
Activity 1: The Peoples of the Thirteen Colonies *(Online)*

Activity 2: History Record Book *(Offline)*

Instructions

Choose either A or B.

A. Written Narration

Write two to four sentences explaining what the lesson was about. If necessary, use the Show You Know questions to help get started. Only include the most important parts of the lesson. Write your name, the date, and the lesson title on your written narration, and put it in your History Record Book.

Sample written narration: "The people in the American colonies came from many lands. There were people from England, Ireland, Germany, and other places. The plantations in the South needed lots of workers. They used slaves from Africa."

B. Picture Narration

Draw a picture of the part of the lesson that interested you most. When you have finished drawing, describe the picture. Below your picture, write a description of what you have drawn. Write your name, the date, and the lesson title on your picture narration, and put it in your History Record Book.

Activity 3: Mapping the Thirteen Colonies *(Offline)*

Instructions

By 1750, there were 13 English colonies along the east coast of North America. Although each colony was a little different from its neighbors, they all had two things in common: they had English laws and English ways of life.

Complete the Mapping the Thirteen Colonies activity sheet to review some of what you've learned about these colonies.

ASSESS

Lesson Assessment: From Many Lands *(Online)*

You will complete an offline assessment covering the main objectives of this lesson. Your learning coach will score this assessment.

LEARN
Activity 4. Optional: From Many Lands *(Online)*

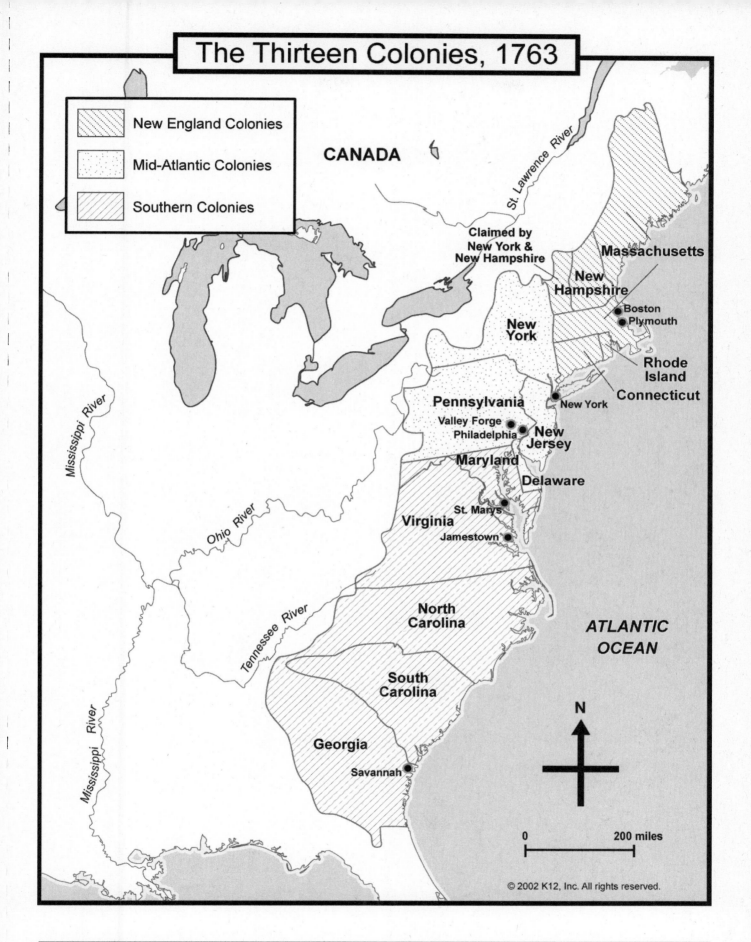

The Thirteen Colonies, 1763

Legend:
- New England Colonies
- Mid-Atlantic Colonies
- Southern Colonies

CANADA

St. Lawrence River

Claimed by New York & New Hampshire

Massachusetts

New Hampshire

- Boston
- Plymouth

New York

Rhode Island

Connecticut

Pennsylvania

- New York

Valley Forge

Philadelphia

New Jersey

Maryland

Delaware

Mississippi River

Ohio River

Virginia

- St. Marys
- Jamestown

Tennessee River

North Carolina

ATLANTIC OCEAN

South Carolina

N

Georgia

- Savannah

0   200 miles

© 2002 K12, Inc. All rights reserved.

Name   Date

Mapping the Thirteen Colonies

Follow the directions in the box below. On the next page, fill in the blanks to show information about four of the colonies.

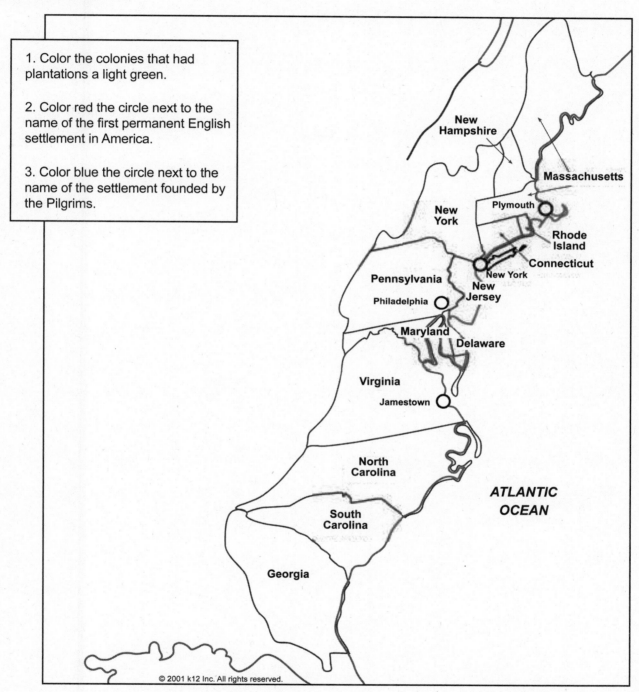

1. Color the colonies that had plantations a light green.

2. Color red the circle next to the name of the first permanent English settlement in America.

3. Color blue the circle next to the name of the settlement founded by the Pilgrims.

New Hampshire

Massachusetts

New York

Plymouth

Rhode Island

Connecticut

New York

Pennsylvania

New Jersey

Philadelphia

Maryland

Delaware

Virginia

Jamestown

North Carolina

ATLANTIC OCEAN

South Carolina

Georgia

Name _____   Date _____

Mapping the Thirteen Colonies

Fill in the blanks to show information about four of the colonies.

New York was originally settled by the _____.

Maryland

Year founded: _____

Founded by _____
Reason for founding:

_____

_____

Pennsylvania

Year founded: _____

Founded by _____
Reason for founding:

_____

_____

Georgia

Year founded: _____

Founded by _____
Reason for founding:

_____

_____

Most of the early colonists were from England, but some colonists came from other countries. Name three countries that some of the colonists came from.

_____

_____

Name_____ Date_____

Lesson Assessment

From Many Lands

1. Who owned New York before the British?_____

2. Besides the English, what other people lived in North

   America?_____

3. What kind of farm required large numbers of workers?_____

4. How did colonists decide to solve the problem of not having enough laborers?_____

Student Guide
Lesson 8: Unit Review and Assessment

You've completed this unit, and now it's time to review what you've learned and take the unit assessment.

Lesson Objectives

- Demonstrate mastery of important knowledge and skills in this unit.
- Demonstrate mastery of important knowledge and skills taught in previous lessons.
- Explain that the first Americans crossed a land bridge to travel from Asia to North America.
- Explain that the Plains Indians hunted buffalo for food and clothing.
- Describe Eastern Woodland tribes as forest dwellers who hunted and farmed.
- Name Jamestown as the first successful English settlement in North America.
- Explain that the English started the Jamestown colony to find gold.
- Identify John Smith as the leader who saved Jamestown.
- Describe the hard experience at Jamestown.
- Describe Plymouth as a colony begun for religious freedom.
- Recognize the key role of the Indians in assisting the Pilgrims through their first year.
- Describe William Penn as the founder of Pennsylvania.
- Explain that Pennsylvania was founded for religious freedom for Quakers and others.
- State that Maryland was founded for religious freedom for Catholics.
- Explain that Georgia was founded as a refuge for debtors.
- State that by the 1730s there were 13 English colonies on the east coast of North America.
- State that New York was originally Dutch.
- Define a plantation as a large farm that required a lot of laborers.
- Explain that African slaves became a large part of the workforce in the South.

PREPARE

Approximate lesson time is 60 minutes.

Materials

    For the Student

        History Record Book

Keywords and Pronunciation

Pueblo (PWEH-bloh)

LEARN
Activity 1: A Look Back *(Offline)*
Instructions

In the last several lessons, we learned about North America and some of the people who called it home before the Europeans arrived. We call these people Native Americans or Indians.

Do you remember how the Native Americans got to America? [1]

After crossing the land bridge from Asia, the newcomers spread all across North America. Their food, shelter, and way of life depended on where they lived. Some fished. Others hunted buffalo. Others grew crops. Can you name two groups of Native Americans we studied? (Hint: These groups are referred to by the areas they lived in.) [2]

In time Native Americans began to notice strangers exploring their coasts. These explorers had sailed all the way from Europe. They began to explore the Atlantic coast of America.

These early European sailors didn't stay long. They just sailed up the coast, stopped here and there, and headed back across the Atlantic. But in time some of the ships didn't leave. The people in the ships came ashore and started to build settlements.

These early settlers were a band of schemers and dreamers. We've just learned about some of them. What country did most of them come from? [3]

What was the name of the first permanent English settlement in North America? (Here's a hint: It was named after the king of England at the time, James I.) [4]

What part of America was Jamestown in? [5]

What was the name of the captain who saved the Jamestown settlement? [6]

The Jamestown settlers came in search of gold. Did they find it? [7]

Other English settlements quickly followed. Lots of different types of English people wanted to leave their country and set up their own colonies in America.

What group sailed on the Mayflower, looking for religious freedom? (Here's a hint: They called their colony Plymouth.) [8]

Why did the Pilgrims leave for America? (This might help: A pilgrim is someone who makes a journey for religious reasons.) [9]

What other group settled in Massachusetts? (This group wanted to "purify" the Church of England.) [10]

Let's move on down the coast of North America to Pennsylvania. Name the man who founded this colony. [11]

Penn and his followers weren't members of the Church of England, either. They belonged to another church called the Society of Friends. But they were usually called by a different name. They got this name because people said they quaked when they prayed. Do you remember what it is? [12]

Let's move further down the coast, to a colony that was founded to be a place where English Catholics and others could worship freely. What was that colony's name? [13]

Let's leapfrog Virginia and go all the way down to Georgia. Whom was this colony set up for? (Here's a clue: These people had been thrown in prison because they couldn't pay their debts.) [14]

In this unit we learned a lot about some of the English colonies. How many colonies were there in all? [15]

How many can you name? Say the names of the colonies you remember. [16]

We call them English colonies because they had English laws and an English way of life. But the English weren't the only ones to live there. Who lived there before the English? [17]

We learned that the English took over New York. Which Europeans had settled in New York before the English took over? [18]

Other Europeans also began arriving in the colonies. Germans began to farm in Pennsylvania, Virginia, and the Carolinas. And the Scotch-Irish settled in the area bordering the Appalachian Mountains.

Another group of people also came to America at this time. They came from Africa, and they did not come by choice. They were brought to America to work as slaves. Most of them were sent to work in the southern colonies, where planters were growing tobacco, indigo, and rice. What do we call the large farms that planters started in the southern colonies? [19]

By 1750, 13 separate British colonies dotted the Atlantic coast. Each colony was a little different from its neighbors. Each one had its own way of doing things. But in time the colonists would see that they had many things in common. Eventually they would think of themselves as American. For many, this thought was nothing short of revolutionary, as we'll see in the lessons ahead.

Activity 2: History Record Book Review (Offline)

Instructions

Use the contents of your History Record Book to review the unit on the World They Found and Founded. Take some time to revisit the narrations, activity sheets, writing activities, and pictures in the History Record Book. Read the narrations aloud. Don't hurry this part of the review; it will refresh your memory and give you a sense of just how much you've already learned.

Activity 3: Online Interactive Review (Online)

ASSESS

Unit Assessment: Unit Review and Assessment (Offline)

Complete an offline Unit Assessment. Your learning coach will score this part of the Assessment.

Name _____   Date _____

The America They Found and Founded

Read each question and its answer choices. Fill in the bubble in front of the word or words that best answer the question.

Questions marked with an asterisk (*) will have more than one correct answer. For these questions, fill in the bubble next to ALL correct answers.

1. How did the first Americans get to North America?
   - ⓐ They rowed in canoes from Africa.
   - ⓑ They walked over a land bridge from Asia.
   - ⓒ They sailed in caravels from Europe.
   - ⓓ They walked over a land bridge from South America.

2. Match each group of Native Americans on the left with a description of the group on the right.

Pacific Northwest	lived in forests; hunted and farmed, grew corn, beans and squash
Southwestern	hunted buffalo for food and clothing
Plains	lived in the desert; grew corn
Eastern Woodland	hunted whales and seals; built large seagoing canoes

3. Why did the English start the Jamestown colony?
   - ⓐ to grow sugarcane
   - ⓑ to spread Christianity
   - ⓒ to find gold
   - ⓓ to grow tobacco

4. Who saved the Jamestown colony from disaster?
   - (a) John Smith
   - (b) William Penn
   - (c) James Oglethorpe
   - (d) George Calvert

5. Complete the table below. In the second column, write the name of the person or group who first settled each colony. In the third column, write the letter for the reason the colony was founded.

William Penn	A. a place where debtors could start over
Pilgrims	B. religious freedom for Catholics
the Dutch	C. religious freedom for Quakers and others
James Oglethorpe	D. to worship God in their own way
Lord George Calvert	E. a place to get rich from the fur trade

Colony	Founded By	Reason for Founding
New York		E.
Plymouth	Pilgrims	
Pennsylvania		
Maryland		
Georgia		

6. Why did African slaves become a large part of the workforce in the American South?
   ⓐ Factories required a lot of workers.
   ⓑ Plantation owners paid high wages.
   ⓒ Plantations required a lot of workers.
   ⓓ Colonists grew a lot of sugarcane.

7. By the 1700s there were _____ English colonies on the east coast of _____.
   ⓐ 13; South America
   ⓑ 13; North America
   ⓒ 10; North America
   ⓓ 15; South America

8. What kind of people settled in the British colonies?
   ⓐ quiet people who obeyed all the British laws
   ⓑ people with unusual ideas who wanted a new start
   ⓒ people from noble families in England and Scotland
   ⓓ fierce warriors who wanted to conquer new lands

9. On the map below, fill in the labels with the following words:

Appalachian   Mississippi   Rocky   Great

10. Which country did most of the colonists in North America come from?

   ⓐ Spain
   ⓑ Portugal
   ⓒ France
   ⓓ England

11. What was the first permanent, successful English settlement in North America?
 ⓐ Jamestown
 ⓑ Plymouth
 ⓒ Pennsylvania
 ⓓ Maryland

12. Which group settled in Massachusetts and wanted to purify the Church of England?
 ⓐ Pilgrims
 ⓑ Puritans
 ⓒ Quakers
 ⓓ Catholics

13. What made it possible for the Pilgrims to make it through their first year in Plymouth?
 ⓐ supply ships from England
 ⓑ help from the Indians
 ⓒ a warm winter with little snow
 ⓓ the discovery of gold

14. In 1750 each of the 13 English colonies was a little different from its neighbor. What was the same about them?
 ⓐ Plantations grew tobacco, rice, and indigo in all the colonies.
 ⓑ The colonies were all settled so that people could have religious freedom.
 ⓒ The colonies all had English laws and an English way of life.
 ⓓ Only English people lived in the thirteen colonies.

15. Number the following events in the order in which they happened.

☐ Georgia is founded as a colony for debtors.

☐ The first Americans cross a land bridge into North America.

☐ The English settle in Jamestown.

* 16. Which of the following are true statements about plantations? (Select **all** that are correct.)
    ⓐ Plantations were small farms.
    ⓑ Plantations existed in the southern colonies.
    ⓒ Plantations required a lot of workers.
    ⓓ Plantation owners hired workers from England.
    ⓔ Plantation owners began using African slaves.

17. Describe the hard experience at Jamestown. Write in complete sentences. Include information about the land, the settlers, the Indians, food, and the weather.

_____

_____

_____

_____

Student Guide
Lesson 1: Reading Graphs

Maps, graphs, and time lines are great tools for showing a lot of information quickly. Maps show places and how people interact with the environment. Graphs are useful for comparing geographic facts and figures. Time lines present important events in the order in which they took place.

Graphs can give you a quick picture of a lot of information.

Lesson Objectives
- Interpret graphs to get information.
- Use time lines to get information.

PREPARE

Approximate lesson time is 60 minutes.

Materials
For the Student
>History Record Book
>Understanding Geography: Map Skills and Our World (Level 3)

Keywords and Pronunciation
bar graph : A chart that uses bars to show how much or how many.
circle graph : A circle-shaped drawing, also called a pie chart, that shows how a whole amount is divided into parts.
graph : A type of drawing used to show how much or how many, or to compare amounts of different things.
picture graph : A kind of drawing, also called a pictograph, that uses pictures to show how much or how many.

LEARN
Activity 1: Graphs *(Online)*
Instructions
- Read and discuss Activity 12: Graphs on pages 52–55 of *Understanding Geography*.
- Answer Questions 1–16 and the Skill Builder Questions on page 55 in your History Record Book.

ASSESS

Lesson Assessment: Reading Graphs (*Online*)
You will complete an online assessment covering the main objectives of this lesson. Your assessment will be scored by the computer.

Student Guide
Lesson 2: Reading a Time Line

A time line is a collection of dates, a bit like a map is a collection of places. Dates on a time line and symbols on a map both represent something bigger. Time lines dates represent important events. Map symbols can represent cities, mountains, and rivers. In some ways, you have to read a time line the way you read a map. They both give you a quick picture of a lot of information.

Lesson Objectives
- Use time lines to get information.
- Make a time line of your life.

PREPARE

Approximate lesson time is 60 minutes.

Materials
For the Student

History Record Book

Understanding Geography: Map Skills and Our World (Level 3)

Keywords and Pronunciation
time line : A line showing dates and events in the order that they happened.

LEARN
Activity 1: Time Lines (Online)
Instructions
- Read and discuss Activity 13: Time Lines on pages 56–59 of Understanding Geography.
- Answer Questions 1–11, 15–20, and Questions 1 and 2 in Skill Builder in your History Record Book.
- Make a time line of a week in your life by following the directions in the Try It Yourself section on page 59.

ASSESS
Lesson Assessment: Reading a Time Line (Online)
You will complete an offline assessment covering the main objectives of this lesson. Your learning coach will score this assessment.

Lesson Assessment

Reading a Time Line

1. **Use the time line on page 58 of** *Understanding Geography* **to answer the following question.**

    Which event happened first?
    - A. Treaty of Paris
    - B. Declaration of Independence

2. **Use the time line on page 58 of** *Understanding Geography* **to answer the following question.**

    Which event happened two years after the signing of the Declaration of Independence?
    - A. Washington started leading the Continent Army
    - B. American soldiers spent the winter at Valley Forge

3. **Use the time line on page 58 of Understanding Geography to answer the following question.**

    The Treaty of Paris officially ended the American Revolution. In what year was it signed?_____

4. **Use the time line on page 56 of** *Understanding Geography* **to answer the following question.**

    When did the Spanish build a fort in St. Augustine, Florida?_____

5. **Use the time line on page 56 of** *Understanding Geography* **to answer the following question.**

    When did the British establish the thirteenth colony, Georgia?_____

Student Guide
Lesson 3: Geography Review and Assessment

You've explored maps and globes, directions and hemispheres, continents, countries, and cities. You've learned about bodies of water, landforms, and how people adapt and use resources. You've learned a lot. Let's take a quick look back before you take the assessment.

Lesson Objectives
- Demonstrate mastery of important knowledge and skills in this unit and the previous unit.
- Demonstrate mastery of important geographic knowledge and skills.

PREPARE

Approximate lesson time is 60 minutes.

LEARN
Activity 1: A Look Back *(Online)*

ASSESS

Lesson Assessment: Geography Review and Assessment (*Online*)
You will complete an online assessment covering the main objectives of this lesson. Your assessment will be scored by the computer.

Student Guide
Lesson 1: English and Proud of It!

- Describe the North American colonies as proud of their English heritage of liberty.
- Explain that American colonists had made laws for the colonies in their own assemblies.
- Explain why American patriots believed that being taxed by Parliament was an attack on their liberty.
- Identify key events and figures in the American Revolution, such as Paul Revere's ride, the Battles of Lexington and Concord, the Declaration of Independence, Valley Forge, French aid, Yorktown, George Washington, and Thomas Jefferson.
- Describe the result of the American Revolution as independence from England and the formation of a modern republic.

English colonists may have been mavericks and even misfits in England, but they were proud to be English. From the Magna Carta to the Glorious Revolution, the British had special regard for rights and liberty. The English monarch did not rule with the absolute power of other kings and queens of Europe. The American Revolution can only be understood in that context.

Lesson Objectives

- Describe the North American colonies as proud of their English heritage of liberty.
- Explain that American colonists had made laws for the colonies in their own assemblies.
- Explain why American patriots believed that being taxed by Parliament was an attack on their liberty.
- Identify key events and figures in the American Revolution, such as Paul Revere's ride, the Battles of Lexington and Concord, the Declaration of Independence, Valley Forge, French aid, Yorktown, George Washington, and Thomas Jefferson.
- Describe the result of the American Revolution as independence from England and the formation of a modern republic.
- Recognize England as a country with a strong concern for liberty.
- Explain that the American colonists had their own assemblies.
- Describe the colonists as proud to be English.

PREPARE

Approximate lesson time is 60 minutes.

Materials

For the Student
- Map of The Thirteen Colonies, 1763
- History Record Book
- paper, 8 1/2" x 11"
- pencils, colored 12

Optional
- If You Lived in Colonial Times by Ann McGovern

Keywords and Pronunciation

assembly : A group of elected representatives who pass laws.

English Parliament (PAHR-luh-muhnt) : The lawmaking body of England, including representatives of the nobility and of the commoners.

liberty : Freedom; the quality of being free.

LEARN
Activity 1: English Liberty, American Freedom (Online)

Activity 2: History Record Book (Online)

Activity 3: Proud to Be English (Online)

ASSESS
Lesson Assessment: English and Proud of It! (Online)

You will complete an offline assessment covering the main objectives of this lesson. Your learning coach will score this assessment.

LEARN
Activity 4. Optional: English and Proud of It! (Offline)
Instructions

Suppose you lived in colonial times. What would your life have been like? To learn more about life in early colonial New England, read *If You Lived in Colonial Times,* written by Ann McGovern and illustrated by June Otani (New York: Scholastic, 1992).

The Thirteen Colonies, 1763

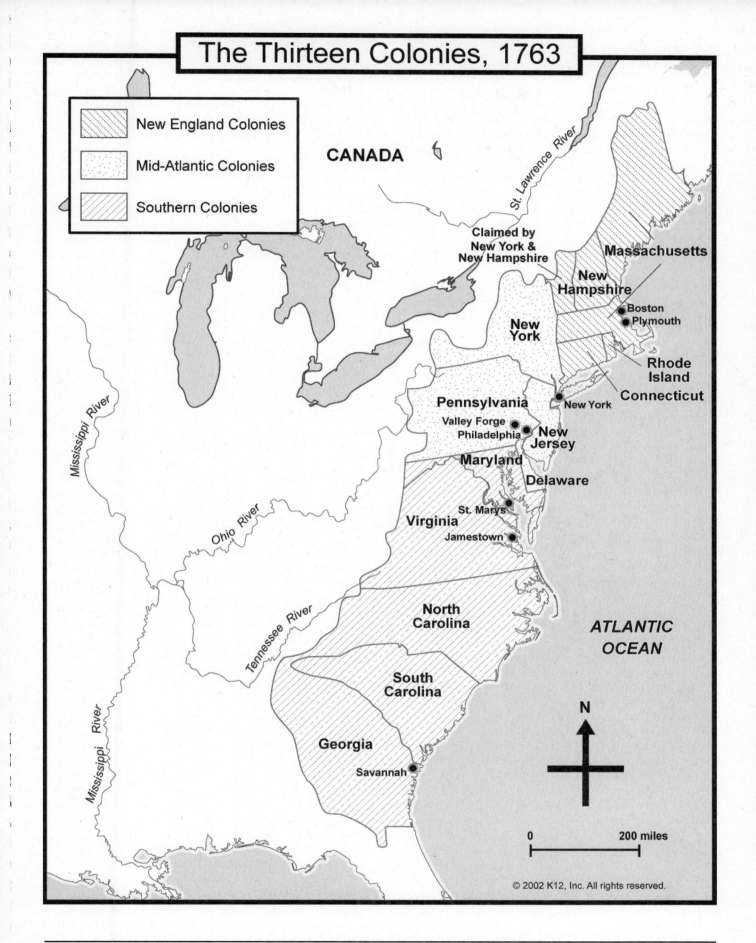

Legend:
- New England Colonies
- Mid-Atlantic Colonies
- Southern Colonies

CANADA

St. Lawrence River

Claimed by New York & New Hampshire

Massachusetts

New Hampshire

Boston
Plymouth

New York

Rhode Island

Connecticut

Pennsylvania

Valley Forge
Philadelphia

New York

New Jersey

Maryland

Delaware

St. Marys

Virginia

Jamestown

North Carolina

South Carolina

Georgia

Savannah

ATLANTIC OCEAN

Mississippi River

Ohio River

Tennessee River

N

0   200 miles

© 2002 K12, Inc. All rights reserved.

Lesson Assessment

English and Proud of It!

1. The English colonists were happy to be among the freest people in the world. What does this

   statement mean?_____

2. How did the colonists pass laws for their colonies?_____

3. Describe the colonists' feelings about being English._____

Student Guide
Lesson 2: No Taxation Without Representation!

England needed to pay its debt from the French and Indian War, so it decided to do something new--tax the colonies directly. The Stamp Act was seen as an attack on American liberty and caused a firestorm of protest. Sam Adams led the resistance in Boston, forming the Sons of Liberty.

Lesson Objectives

- State that American colonists objected to the Stamp Act.
- Explain the phrase "no taxation without representation."
- Identify Samuel Adams as an American patriot.
- Describe the Sons of Liberty as a group formed by Samuel Adams to oppose the British tax.

PREPARE

Approximate lesson time is 60 minutes.

Materials

    For the Student
        History Record Book
        paper, 8 1/2" x 11"
        pencils, colored 12

Keywords and Pronunciation

patriot (PAY-tree-uht) : A person who loves and supports his or her country.

LEARN
Activity 1: Putting a Stamp on Freedom (Online)

Activity 2: History Record Book (Offline)

Instructions

Choose either A or B.

A. Written Narration

Write two to four sentences explaining what the lesson was about. If necessary, use the Show You Know questions to help get started. Only include the most important parts of the lesson. Write your name, the date, and the lesson title on your written narration, and put it in your History Record Book.

Sample written narration: "The colonists were angry because Parliament was trying to tax them with the Stamp Act. The colonists didn't like the tax because they didn't get to vote on it. They said, 'No taxation without representation.'"

B. Picture Narration

Draw a picture of the part of the lesson that interested you most. When you have finished drawing, describe the picture. Below your picture, write a description of what you have drawn. Write your name, the date, and the lesson title on your picture narration, and put it in your History Record Book.

Activity 3: Stamping Out Taxation *(Offline)*
Instructions

The English Parliament decided to raise some of the money to pay for the French and Indian War by taxing the colonists. They passed the Stamp Act in 1765. This law required the colonists to pay money to put special stamps on all the paper products they used. Buying the stamps was really the same as paying a tax.

But the colonists did not have a chance to vote on whether they wanted to pay this tax. They were angry and complained a lot. "No taxation without representation!" they said.

Here are some examples of actual stamps. Look carefully at them. Then create a poster showing that the colonists protested this tax and did not want to pay it. Think about Samuel Adams, the Sons of Liberty, and the idea of taxation without representation. Plan your poster using drawing paper. Then enlarge it on poster board if you wish.

ASSESS

Lesson Assessment: No Taxation Without Representation! (*Online*)

You will complete an offline assessment covering the main objectives of this lesson. Your learning coach will score this assessment.

LEARN

Activity 4. Optional: No Taxation Without Representation! (*Offline*)

Instructions

Imagine that Hannah had a chance to meet Samuel Adams at the Liberty Tree. Draw a series of four pictures showing their meeting. Be sure to include speech balloons showing their conversation about the Stamp Act, the Sons of Liberty, and the idea of taxation without representation.

Name_____   Date_____

Lesson Assessment

No Taxation Without Representation!

1. What did the colonists think of the Stamp Act?_____

2. What did "no taxation without representation" mean?_____

3. How would you describe Samuel Adams?_____

4. What did Samuel Adams do?_____

5. Who were the Sons of Liberty and what were they fighting

   against?_____

Student Guide
Lesson 3: The First Clashes

By 1770, new taxes from England, and British troops sent to keep order, made the colonists worry about their future and the future of liberty in America. The Boston Massacre seemed to confirm their fears. They organized resistance, forming the minutemen and hosting what would become known as the Boston Tea Party.

Lesson Objectives

- Explain that the colonists resented the presence of British troops in their cities.
- Describe the minutemen as Americans who could be ready to fight in a minute.
- Identify the Boston Massacre as a clash between colonists and British soldiers.
- Explain that during the Boston Tea Party colonists threw tea into the harbor to protest the tea tax.

PREPARE

Approximate lesson time is 60 minutes.

Materials

For the Student
> The Revolutionary War by Brendan January
> History Record Book
> paper, 8 1/2" x 11"
> pencils, colored 12

Optional
> Boston Tea Party by Richard Conrad Stein

LEARN
Activity 1: Tea Overboard! *(Offline)*
Instructions
Get Ready

What country ruled the American colonies in 1765? [1]

Which tax made the American colonists especially angry that year? [2]

What phrase did colonists use to explain why they objected to that tax? [3]

What did that mean? [4]

Who led the resistance to the Stamp Act in Boston? [5]

What did he do to get England to change its mind? [6]

How quickly things seemed to change between the American colonists and the British. In 1763 most Americans were proud of George III, happy to have won the war against the French, and happy that Britain now had so much new land in North America. But five years later many things had changed.

You've learned about the new taxes from Britain. Sam Adams and colonists in Massachusetts protested against them. Colonists in Virginia, New York, and Pennsylvania did, too. They were angry. Why? Because they didn't think they should pay taxes? No. They were angry because they were being taxed without their consent. They had no representatives in Parliament. No one asked them what they thought.

The colonists said, "No taxation without representation!" If Parliament could tax them now, then when would it end? How much of their money would Parliament be able to take away? The colonists feared they could lose their livelihood and their freedom.

The colonists were not a quiet bunch. They protested and even rioted! They said, "No way, King George!" And the king cleared his throat and said, "This has to stop! We must keep order. Send the redcoats to Boston and New York."

The redcoats were British soldiers. They wore bright red coats as part of their uniform. When the American colonists saw the British redcoats, they turned bright red, too. How dare King George and Parliament treat their own people like a conquered enemy! How dare they send redcoats with muskets to keep order in Boston and New York!

Let's find out what happened next.

Read pages 10 to 15 of *The Revolutionary War,* by Brendan January.

After you have read the selection, come back to answer the Show You Know questions.

Show You Know

What did the colonists think about having the redcoats in Boston and New York? [1]

Who were the minutemen? [2]

In 1770, some colonists were killed when redcoats fired their muskets into an angry crowd in Boston. What is that clash between the redcoats and colonists called? [3]

How did Boston colonists protest the tax on tea? [4]

What was that event called? [5]

How did the British get even for the Boston Tea Party? [6]

Activity 2: History Record Book (Offline)

Instructions

Choose either A or B.

A. Written Narration

Write two to four sentences explaining what the lesson was about. If necessary, use the Show You Know questions to help get started. Only include the most important parts of the lesson. Write your name, the date, and the lesson title on your written narration, and put it in your History Record Book.

Sample written narration: "The colonists did not like it when the king sent the redcoats to their cities. The Boston Massacre happened when some redcoats shot some colonists. Then the colonists decided to protest the tax on tea by throwing tea into the harbor. This was the Boston Tea Party."

B. Picture Narration

Draw a picture of the part of the lesson that interested you most. When you have finished drawing, describe the picture. Below your picture, write a description of what you have drawn. Write your name, the date, and the lesson title on your picture narration, and put it in your History Record Book.

Activity 3: Not a Party *(Offline)*
Instructions

The Boston Tea Party wasn't a party, and no tea was served. It was really a protest demonstration by the colonists. They didn't want to pay the tax on tea, so a group of men dressed as Mohawk Indians boarded a ship and tossed 342 chests of tea overboard.

After this, the British decided to send more soldiers--redcoats--to Boston and New York. Now many of the colonists were angry about both the tax and the soldiers. They wanted the whole world to know it, and they wanted others to join their protest.

Help the colonists gain support by creating a brochure that shows what they were protesting. Illustrate some of the things the colonists did not like about the actions the British had taken. Then write a paragraph asking others to join or support the fight against the actions of the British soldiers and Parliament.

ASSESS
Lesson Assessment: The First Clashes (*Online*)

You will complete an offline assessment covering the main objectives of this lesson. Your learning coach will score this assessment.

LEARN
Activity 4. Optional: The First Clashes *(Offline)*
Instructions

Learn more about the Boston Tea Party by reading the book of the same name by Richard Conrad Stein (Chicago: Children's Press, 1998). Investigate the people behind the events, and explore what really happened on that fateful night of December 16, 1773.

Lesson Assessment

The First Clashes

1. What did the colonists think about having the redcoats in Boston and New
   York?_____

2. Who were the minutemen?_____

3. In 1770, some colonists were killed when redcoats fired their muskets into an angry crowd in
   Boston. What is that clash between the redcoats and colonists called._____

4. How did Boston colonists protest the tax on tea?_____

5. What was the event called when the colonists threw tea into Boston harbor in
   protest?_____

Student Guide
Lesson 4: Lexington, Concord, and Bunker Hill

The Revolutionary War began before Americans declared independence. Warned by Paul Revere, American farmers at Lexington and Concord faced the British redcoats in battle for the first time. Two months later, at the Battle of Bunker Hill, the two groups clashed again.

Lesson Objectives

- Identify Paul Revere as the person who warned colonists of the approach of British troops.
- Describe Lexington and Concord as the first battles against the British in the Revolutionary War.
- State that the minutemen fought the British soldiers from behind stone walls and trees.
- Explain that in the first battles, the patriots showed they could and would fight.

PREPARE

Approximate lesson time is 60 minutes.

Materials

For the Student

The Revolutionary War by Brendan January

History Record Book

crayons 8

paper, 8 1/2" x 11"

pencils, colored 12

Optional

paper, notebook

LEARN
Activity 1: Paul Revere Delivers a Warning *(Offline)*

Instructions
Get Ready

How did the Americans feel about redcoats in Boston and New York? [1]

What was it called when the redcoats fired on a Boston crowd? [2]

How did Bostonians protest the tea tax? [3]

Why did they form the minutemen? [4]

The American colonists had thrown tea into Boston's harbor. Now the British were angry. King George thought it was time to teach those rebellious colonists a lesson. So he closed the port of Boston. "No more trade for the merchants of Massachusetts!" Then he took some powers away from the Massachusetts Assembly. "Don't think you're going to run your own government anymore." Then he said, "By the way, Bostonians, you have to let the redcoats live in your homes and feed them, too."

All this was too much for the colonists. In and around Boston, they started collecting gunpowder and storing weapons. The minutemen were training harder. Maybe they would actually fight the redcoats to get the king to recognize their rights!

Now, at this time--which was 1774--most American colonists were thinking, "OK, maybe we'll fight a little and then the king will understand we have rights. We'll prove we're strong. Parliament will never tax us again. We'll pass our own laws and taxes with our assemblies, and we'll go back to being part of the British Empire." Americans were not yet thinking, "Let's become our own country." The idea of independence didn't become popular until after the war began. Let's read about that.

Read pages 16 to 23 of *The Revolutionary War,* by Brendan January.

After you have read the selection, come back to answer the Show You Know questions.

Show You Know

Who rode through the country to warn the colonists that the British were coming? [1]

Why were the Battles of Lexington and Concord important? [2]

Who fought against the British soldiers from behind stone walls and trees? [3]

What did the Battles of Lexington and Concord and the Battle of Bunker Hill show the British about the Americans? [4]

Activity 2: History Record Book (Offline)

Instructions

Choose either A or B.

A. Written Narration

Write two to four sentences explaining what the lesson was about. If necessary, use the Show You Know questions to help get started. Only include the most important parts of the lesson. Write your name, the date, and the lesson title on your written narration, and put it in your History Record Book.

Sample written narration: "The British sent redcoats to Lexington, but Paul Revere galloped ahead on his horse to warn the colonists. The colonists and the British fought at Lexington and Concord. These were the first battles of the Revolutionary War. The minutemen showed the British they were ready to fight."

B. Picture Narration

Draw a picture of the part of the lesson that interested you most. When you have finished drawing, describe the picture. Below your picture, write a description of what you have drawn. Write your name, the date, and the lesson title on your picture narration, and put it in your History Record Book.

Activity 3: Paul Revere's Midnight Ride (Online)

ASSESS

Lesson Assessment: Lexington, Concord, and Bunker Hill (Online)

You will complete an offline assessment covering the main objectives of this lesson. Your learning coach will score this assessment.

LEARN

Activity 4. Optional: Lexington, Concord, and Bunker Hill (Online)

Write your own "Today in History" to describe the Battle of Bunker Hill.

Lesson Assessment

Lexington, Concord, and Bunker Hill

1. Who rode through the country to warn the colonists that the British were

   coming?_____

2. Why were the Battles of Lexington and Concord important?_____

3. Who fought against the British soldiers from behind stone walls and trees?_____

4. What did the Battles of Lexington and Concord and the Battle of Bunker Hill show the British about

   the Americans?_____

Student Guide
Lesson 5: The Declaration of Independence

In July 1776, American patriots made a bold move. The colonies voted for independence from Great Britain.

Lesson Objectives

- Describe the Declaration of Independence as the document that announced America's separation from England and the formation of a new country.
- State that the Declaration of Independence announced the formation of a new country named the United States of America.
- Identify July 4, 1776, as America's Independence Day.
- Explain that the Liberty Bell was the bell rung to celebrate American independence.
- Identify the Liberty Bell from a picture.

PREPARE

Approximate lesson time is 60 minutes.

Materials

For the Student
    History Record Book
    paper, notebook

LEARN
Activity 1: Independence Rings! *(Online)*

Activity 2: History Record Book *(Online)*

Activity 3: Declaring Independence *(Online)*

ASSESS

Lesson Assessment: The Declaration of Independence (*Online*)

You will complete an offline assessment covering the main objectives of this lesson. Your learning coach will score this assessment.

LEARN
Activity 4. Optional: The Declaration of Independence *(Online)*

Name _____   Date _____

Lesson Assessment

The Declaration of Independence

1. What was the Declaration of Independence? _____

2. What is the name of the new country the colonies formed with the Declaration of

   Independence? _____

3. What is the date of America's Independence Day? _____

4. What is the Liberty Bell? _____

5. Which of the following shows a picture of the Liberty Bell?

A.   B.   C.

Student Guide
Lesson 6: Crossing the Delaware and Getting Help from the French

After many defeats, Washington surprised the British at Trenton with his bold Christmas night crossing of the Delaware. Later, the victory at Saratoga brought the French into the war.

Lesson Objectives

- Describe some obstacles to American victory in the Revolutionary War.
- Identify the scene of Washington crossing the Delaware.
- Explain the importance of Washington crossing the Delaware.
- State that the French fought on the side of the Americans in the Revolutionary War.

PREPARE

Approximate lesson time is 60 minutes.

Materials

For the Student

The Revolutionary War by Brendan January

History Record Book

paper, 8 1/2" x 11"

Optional

paint, watercolor, 8 colors or more

paintbrush

Keywords and Pronunciation

Hessians (HEH-shuhns)

John Burgoyne (bur-GOYN)

LEARN
Activity 1: Famous Battles and New Friends (Offline)
Instructions
Get Ready

What happened on July 4, 1776? [1]

Who wrote the Declaration of Independence? [2]

Who got all 13 colonies to agree that declaring independence was a good idea? [3]

Who was put in charge of the American army to lead the war? [4]

Was the American army in good shape? [5]

Declaring independence from Great Britain was a bold move. Americans were saying, "We will be our own country. We will fight the British for our freedom, and we will fight until we win."

Until we win! Would that be possible? England had the best navy in the world. It had one of the best armies in the world. The British had defeated the French and Spanish in war. Why shouldn't they defeat the Americans, too? After all, these rebels were colonial farmers, not soldiers!

When independence was declared, General George Washington was already commanding the poorly equipped American army. Washington worked hard to find weapons and uniforms for his troops. He worked hard to train them.

Today's reading tells us about the course of the war. The reading starts in March 1776, a little before the Declaration of Independence. Let's see what George Washington did.

Read pages 26 through 32 of *The Revolutionary War,* by Brendan January. After finishing page 32, answer the following questions.

- Why could Washington surprise the British and Hessians? [1]
- Why was that surprise victory so important to the Americans? [2]

Now read pages 33 through 37. After finishing page 37, answer the following questions.

- What were the French waiting for before helping the Americans in the Revolutionary War? [3]
- How was the British General Burgoyne surprised at Saratoga? [4]
- In 1778, which nation agreed to help the American patriots? [5]

After you have read the selections, come back to answer the Show You Know questions.

Show You Know

What were some things that made it hard for Americans to win the Revolutionary War? [1]

If you see a picture of General Washington crossing an icy river in a boat with his men, what scene are you looking at? [2]

What happened when Washington launched that surprise attack on Christmas night? [3]

Why was it important that Washington crossed the Delaware and attacked successfully? [4]

Which European nation eventually agreed to help the United States fight the British? [5]

Activity 2: History Record Book (Offline)

Instructions

Choose either A or B.

A. Written Narration

Write two to four sentences explaining what the lesson was about. If necessary, use the Show You Know questions to help get started. Only include the most important parts of the lesson. Write your name, the date, and the lesson title on your written narration, and put it in your History Record Book.

Sample written narration: "Americans didn't know whether they could win a war against England. They didn't think their army was as good as the British army. Then Washington crossed the Delaware and beat the British. That gave the Americans hope."

B. Picture Narration

Draw a picture of the part of the lesson that interested you most. When you have finished drawing, describe the picture. Below your picture, write a description of what you have drawn. Write your name, the date, and the lesson title on your picture narration, and put it in your History Record Book.

Activity 3: Painting the Revolutionary War *(Online)*

ASSESS

Lesson Assessment: Crossing the Delaware and Getting Help from the French *(Online)*

You will complete an offline assessment covering the main objectives of this lesson. Your learning coach will score this assessment.

LEARN

Activity 4. Optional: Crossing the Delaware and Getting Help from the French *(Online)*

Name_____   Date_____

Lesson Assessment Key

Crossing the Delaware and Getting Help from the French

1. What were some things that made it hard for Americans to win the Revolutionary

   War?_____

2. If you see a picture of General Washington crossing an icy river in a boat with his men, what scene

   are you looking at?_____

3. Why was it important that Washington crossed the Delaware and attacked

   successfully?_____

4. Which European nation eventually agreed to help the United States fight the

   British?_____

Student Guide
Lesson 7: Winter at Valley Forge

In winter of 1777-1778, George Washington and his men endured great hardship at their camp at Valley Forge. Suffering from terrible cold, without enough food, clothing, or shelter, many died. Washington trained his men through the winter, and the American army emerged stronger in the spring.

Lesson Objectives

- Describe the winter at Valley Forge as a time of great hardship.
- Explain that many men suffered from the cold and the lack of food, clothing, and shelter.
- Describe Washington as the leader who got the soldiers through the winter and trained them to be a better army.

PREPARE

Approximate lesson time is 60 minutes.

Materials

For the Student

History Record Book

💻 Why Valley Forge? activity sheet

Keywords and Pronunciation

von Steuben (vahn STOO-buhn)

LEARN
Activity 1: A Cold, Harsh Winter *(Online)*

Activity 2: History Record Book *(Offline)*

Instructions

Choose either A or B.

A. Written Narration

Write two to four sentences explaining what the lesson was about. If necessary, use the Show You Know questions to help get started. Only include the most important parts of the lesson. Write your name, the date, and the lesson title on your written narration, and put it in your History Record Book.

Sample written narration: "The American army spent a bad winter at Valley Forge. They did not have much to eat or wear. It was cold and they had to live in the snow. George Washington helped them get through the winter."

B. Picture Narration

Draw a picture of the part of the lesson that interested you most. When you have finished drawing, describe the picture. Below your picture, write a description of what you have drawn. Write your name, the date, and the lesson title on your picture narration, and put it in your History Record Book.

Activity 3: Why Valley Forge? *(Offline)*
Instructions

Did you wonder why the Americans chose Valley Forge? One reason was that Valley Forge was located on a high plateau, which meant that attackers would have had an uphill climb to reach it. There were also two nearby creeks, which attackers would have to cross to reach the camp. But one of Valley Forge's best features was that the plateau was on a river that helped protect it.

What river? Review the lesson, answer the questions on the Why Valley Forge? activity sheet, and spell out its name.

Then, if you decide want to learn more about the challenges the Continental Army faced, visit your library or bookstore. Here are some possible sources:

The Winter of Red Snow: The Revolutionary War Diary of Abigail Jane Stewart, by Kristiana Gregory (New York: Scholastic, 1996)

The Winter at Valley Forge: Survival and Victory (Adventures in Colonial America), by James E. Knight with illustrations by George Guzzi (Mahwah, NJ: Troll Communications, 1999)

Winter at Valley Forge by Edward F. Dolan Jr. (Tarrytown, NY: Marshall Cavendish, 2001)

ASSESS
Lesson Assessment: Winter at Valley Forge (*Online*)
You will complete an offline assessment covering the main objectives of this lesson. Your learning coach will score this assessment.

LEARN
Activity 4. Optional: Winter at Valley Forge *(Online)*

Name _____   Date _____

Why Valley Forge

Fill in the blanks with the correct answers. Then put the boxed letters in order in the spaces at the bottom to spell out the name of the river that helped protect the Americans during the winter of 1777–78.

1. What is the name of the place in New York where the Americans defeated the British in October 1777?

   ☐ _ _ _ _ _ _ _

2. What was the name for the American army?

   ☐ _ _ _ _ _ _ _ _ _ _ _ Army

3. Who was the general of that army?

   _ _ _ _ _ _ _ _ _ ☐ _ _ _ _ _

4. What is another name for the diaries that several soldiers kept?

   _ _ ☐ _ _ _ _ _

5. What is the name of the colony where Valley Forge was located?

   _ _ _ _ _ ☐ ☐ _ _ _ _

6. How did the Americans get to Valley Forge?

   They _ _ _ ☐ _ _ .

7. What happened to some 2,000 of the American soldiers during this winter?

   They _ ☐ _ _ .

8. Where were the redcoats during this time?

   _ _ _ ☐ _ _ _ ☐ _ _ _ _

9. What was the name of the river that helped protect the camp at Valley Forge?

   ☐ ☐ ☐ ☐ ☐ ☐ ☐ ☐ ☐ ☐ River

Name _____   Date _____

Lesson Assessment

Winter at Valley Forge

1. How would you describe the soldiers' experience at Valley Forge during the winter of 1777-
   1778?_____

2. What were some of the problems the soldiers faced?_____

3. Who was the leader who helped the American troops survive during the winter of 1777-
   1778?_____

Student Guide
Lesson 8: Victory at Yorktown

The Battle of Yorktown, the last great battle of the American Revolution, secured victory for the Americans. Aided by the French, Washington's army defeated the army of Cornwallis. In 1783, the young United States of America signed a peace treaty with England.

Lesson Objectives

- Describe the battle at Yorktown, Virginia, as the last great battle of the Revolutionary War.
- Identify Cornwallis as the general who surrendered to Washington.
- Explain that the French blockade helped secure victory.
- Identify the form of government of the United States as a republic.

PREPARE

Approximate lesson time is 60 minutes.

Materials

For the Student

The Revolutionary War by Brendan January

History Record Book

🖥 Cornwallis Surrenders activity sheet

pencils, colored 12

Optional

The World Turned Upside Down: George Washington and the Battle of Yorktown by Richard Ferrie

Keywords and Pronunciation

republic : a government in which citizens elect representatives to make the laws and help see that they are followed

LEARN
Activity 1: The Revolution Ends *(Offline)*
Instructions
Get Ready

Where did American soldiers camp in that dreadful winter of 1777-1778? [1]

What were some of the hardships the Americans faced that winter? [2]

Whose courage and determination got the Americans through at Valley Forge? [3]

What country gave the Americans hope in the spring of 1778 when it decided to help them? [4]

In the spring of 1778, American soldiers recovered from their long, hard winter at Valley Forge. There was much to cheer them. The French were sending ships and men to fight alongside the Americans. And the army was getting better food and weapons.

The British were worried about the French who were on the way. So they abandoned Philadelphia. The British decided they would concentrate their fighting in the South. They thought many Americans in the southern states were still loyal to Great Britain. Maybe it would be easier to fight the rebels there.

Let's find out what happened when another British general, Charles Cornwallis, decided to invade the south. Read pages 39 to 43 of *The Revolutionary War,* by Brendan January. After you have read the selection, come back to read the follow-up text and answer the Show You Know questions.

When Americans signed the peace treaty with Great Britain in September 1783, they knew they had won a great victory. For the first time in history, British colonists had rebelled against and defeated the mighty British Empire.

Americans had been proud to be British until the king and Parliament started taking away their liberties. Now they were proud to be Americans. They shouted to all who would listen that they were free and independent! Now they didn't just call their war against Britain a war for independence. They called it a *revolution*--a war that announced a really big change.

The American Revolution had been long and hard. The young nation had fought for eight years. Now it was time to stop fighting and start building. What would Americans build? What kind of government would they have?

Americans were sure they wanted to rule themselves. There was no king in the colonies and there were no nobles. For a long time colonists had elected representatives to their own assemblies. They thought it was time that ordinary people started running their own lives.

So the Americans of 1776 launched a bold new experiment. They made the United States of America a republic. Do you remember what a *republic* is? It's a government in which citizens elect representatives to make the laws and help see that they are followed. Nobody is born with power in a republic. You have to earn it with votes from fellow citizens.

You might say there was nothing so new about a republic. After all, Rome had a republic. So did Florence in the Renaissance and some other Italian city-states. But those republics were many years in the past. Now, in this New World called the Americas, the United States was a place where people could rule themselves.

Would it work? Everyone knew that republics didn't have a good chance of succeeding. The republic of Rome had crumbled. The republic of Florence did, too. Could people get along without kings and nobles?

That's next year's story. For now, Americans had won their war for independence. Fireworks exploded. Bells rang. Huzzahs and hurrahs filled the air. The future was filled with hope.

Show You Know

What was the last great battle of the American Revolution? [1]

Which British general was defeated at Yorktown and surrendered to Washington? [2]

Which country's naval blockade helped win the battle at Yorktown? [3]

Why did the British pipers play *The World Turned Upside Down* when they surrendered to George Washington? [4]

What treaty officially ended the Revolutionary War? [5]

What kind of government did the Americans decide to form? [6]

Activity 2: History Record Book *(Offline)*
Instructions

Choose either A or B.

A. Written Narration
Write two to four sentences explaining what the lesson was about. If necessary, use the Show You Know questions to help get started. Only include the most important parts of the lesson. Write your name, the date, and the lesson title on your written narration, and put it in your History Record Book.

Sample written narration: "Yorktown was the last great battle of the American Revolution. Cornwallis led the British army. They had to surrender to the Americans. The French helped beat the British at Yorktown with their ships."

B. Picture Narration
Draw a picture of the part of the lesson that interested you most. When you have finished drawing, describe the picture. Below your picture, write a description of what you have drawn. Write your name, the date, and the lesson title on your picture narration, and put it in your History Record Book.

Activity 3: Color the United States Victorious *(Online)*

ASSESS
Lesson Assessment: Victory at Yorktown (*Online*)
You will complete an offline assessment covering the main objectives of this lesson. Your learning coach will score this assessment.

LEARN
Activity 4. Optional: Victory at Yorktown *(Offline)*
Instructions
Learn more of the details about the famous battle that ended the Revolutionary War. Read *The World Turned Upside Down: George Washington and the Battle of Yorktown,* by Richard Ferrie (New York: Holiday House, 1999).

Name _____   Date _____

Surrender of Cornwallis

Color your own copy of John Trumbull's painting, *Surrender of Cornwallis*. Label the French soldiers, the British soldiers, General Benjamin Lincoln, General George Washington, and the American soldiers near Washington on horseback and on foot.

Lesson Assessment

Victory at Yorktown

1. What was the last great battle of the American Revolution?_____

2. Which British general was defeated at Yorktown and surrendered to Washington?_____

3. Which country's naval blockade helped win the battle at Yorktown?_____

4. What kind of government did the Americans decide to form?_____

Student Guide
Lesson 9: Unit Review and Assessment

You've completed this unit, and now it's time to review what you've learned and take the unit assessment.

Lesson Objectives

- Demonstrate mastery of important knowledge and skills in this unit.
- Explain that the American colonists had their own assemblies.
- Describe the colonists as proud to be English.
- State that American colonists objected to the Stamp Act.
- Explain the phrase "no taxation without representation."
- Identify Samuel Adams as an American patriot.
- Explain that the colonists resented the presence of British troops in their cities.
- Describe the minutemen as Americans who could be ready to fight in a minute.
- Identify the Boston Massacre as a clash between colonists and British soldiers.
- Explain that during the Boston Tea Party colonists threw tea into the harbor to protest the tea tax.
- Identify Paul Revere as the person who warned colonists of the approach of British troops.
- Describe Lexington and Concord as the first battles against the British in the Revolutionary War.
- State that the Declaration of Independence announced the formation of a new country named the United States of America.
- Identify July 4, 1776, as America's Independence Day.
- Explain that the Liberty Bell was the bell rung to celebrate American independence.
- Describe some obstacles to American victory in the Revolutionary War.
- Explain the importance of Washington crossing the Delaware.
- State that the French fought on the side of the Americans in the Revolutionary War.
- Describe the winter at Valley Forge as a time of great hardship.
- Explain that many men suffered from the cold and the lack of food, clothing, and shelter.
- Describe Washington as the leader who got the soldiers through the winter and trained them to be a better army.
- Describe the battle at Yorktown, Virginia, as the last great battle of the Revolutionary War.
- Identify Cornwallis as the general who surrendered to Washington.
- Explain that the French blockade helped secure victory.
- Identify the form of government of the United States as a republic.

PREPARE

Approximate lesson time is 60 minutes.

Materials

> For the Student
>> History Record Book

Keywords and Pronunciation

English Parliament (PAHR-luh-muhnt) : The lawmaking body of England, including representatives of the nobility and of the commoners.

LEARN

Activity 1: A Look Back *(Offline)*

Instructions

A revolution is a very big change. You've been studying the American Revolution. As you've learned, it caused a *huge* change, even though the American colonists didn't start out wanting huge change.

Let's review. At the end of the French and Indian War, were Americans tired of being British? Did they hate England and want to be independent? [1]

Everyone knew that the English were the freest people in the world. They had the Magna Carta. They had the Glorious Revolution. They had rights! The English were special, and so were the English colonies. That's why the colonists were proud to be English.

Most American colonists experienced English liberty firsthand. That's because for most of their history, the king and Parliament didn't worry too much about the colonies. Colonists in Pennsylvania, Massachusetts, Virginia, and elsewhere set up their own assemblies and elected their own representatives. They passed their own laws and taxed themselves. The colonists respected the king and Parliament, but didn't spend a lot of time thinking about them. The 13 English colonies had a lot of liberty.

Then things changed. Do you remember why? After the French and Indian War the British had bills to pay. The king needed money. Where could he get it? Why, the colonies, of course. The British Parliament started passing laws taxing the colonists.

The colonists were angry. They weren't represented in Parliament! They were only represented in their colonial assemblies. The colonists said they should not be taxed by a legislature in which they had no representative. What was the famous phrase they used to express this idea? [2]

The Americans even had a little tea party to convince the British they were upset about being taxed by Parliament. What was the Boston Tea Party? [3]

What started as an argument about taxes became a fight about rights and liberty. Eventually, the colonists became convinced that the king and Parliament wanted to take away their rights and liberties. They stored some weapons in case they needed to fight. They trained themselves to be ready to fight with only a minute's warning. The minutemen and the Sons of Liberty prepared for battle.

When Paul Revere rode into the countryside on Apri 18, 1775, he warned American patriots that the redcoats were coming to take away their weapons. On the next day, redcoats and patriots fought the first battle of the American Revolution. Do you remember what it was called? [4]

American minutemen shot from behind trees and turned the British back. More shooting followed. Two months later, at Bunker Hill, the Americans lost a battle but showed the British they meant business.

All this fighting happened before a very important document was written. The colonists were still arguing about whether to declare independence. Where did the representatives of the colonies meet to decide whether to declare independence? [5]

John Adams and Thomas Jefferson worked hard to make independence happen. Do you remember why the date July 4, 1776, is important? [6]

The colonists voted in favor of making the United States of America its own country. What is the name of the document that established the United States of America as a nation? [7]

A long, hard war followed the Declaration of Independence. After all, the Americans were fighting the English, who had a well-trained army and the strongest navy in the world. The Americans were just a bunch of liberty-loving farmers!

Fortunately, the American army had a wonderful leader. His name was George Washington. Whether he was leading his men across the icy Delaware and surprising the sleeping British, or making his army better through that terrible winter at Valley Forge, George Washington was "the indispensable man." People later said that without him, the American Revolution wouldn't have succeeded.

But it did succeed. At Yorktown in 1781, the world turned upside down. The British surrendered to the Americans! For the first time in history, an old world nation (England) was forced to free its colonies in the New World. A group of colonists made their own country, the United States of America. They decided they would rule it themselves. The new United States became not a new monarchy, but the first modern republic! These were huge changes. But the biggest change was that in time, people from all over the world would start thinking about self-government, democracy, and independence. What would this mean for the Spanish colonies in South America? What would it mean for those who lived under kings in Europe? It would mean a lot. But that's next year's story.

Activity 2: History Record Book Review *(Offline)*

Instructions

Use the contents of your History Record Book to review the unit on the American Revolution. Take some time to revisit the narrations, activity sheets, writing activities, and pictures in the History Record Book. Read the narrations aloud. Don't hurry this part of the review; it will refresh your memory and give you a sense of just how much you've already learned.

Activity 3: Online Interactive Review *(Online)*

ASSESS

Unit Assessment: The American Revolution (*Offline*)

Complete an offline Unit Assessment. Your learning coach will score this part of the Assessment.

Name _____   Date _____

The American Revolution

Read each question and its answer choices. Fill in the bubble in front of the word or words that best answer the question.

Questions marked with an asterisk (*) will have more than one correct answer. For these questions, fill in the bubble next to ALL correct answers.

1. Which of the following best describes the American colonists in 1763?
   - ⓐ They were unhappy with England and wanted to be free.
   - ⓑ They were proud of their rights and liberties and proud to be English.
   - ⓒ They were embarrassed to be called "English" because they had few rights.
   - ⓓ They hated King George III and wanted their independence from England.

2. Who made most of the laws for the individual American colonies before 1763?
   - ⓐ British Parliament
   - ⓑ colonial assemblies
   - ⓒ courts
   - ⓓ presidents

3. When the British Parliament passed the Stamp Act, American colonists protested, saying, "_____!"
   - ⓐ Remember the Alamo!
   - ⓑ Don't tread on me!
   - ⓒ No taxation without representation!
   - ⓓ Let my people go!

4. Why didn't Americans agree with the Stamp Act?
   - (a) They were being taxed without their consent.
   - (b) They didn't like the images on the stamps.
   - (c) They wanted the British Parliament to tax them.
   - (d) They were cheap and didn't want to pay any taxes.

5. What happened during the Boston Tea Party?
   - (a) Colonists drank 25 barrels of Boston tea under the Liberty Tree.
   - (b) Minutemen attacked British soldiers to keep them from entering Boston.
   - (c) British redcoats fired their muskets at a group of colonists in Boston.
   - (d) Colonists dumped tea into Boston Harbor to protest the tax on it.

6. What document announced to the world that Britain's American colonies were separating from England and becoming their own country?
   - (a) Magna Carta
   - (b) Declaration of Independence
   - (c) English Bill of Rights
   - (d) Stamp Act

7. What country fought on the side of the colonists during the Revolutionary War?
   - (a) Spain
   - (b) Portugal
   - (c) France
   - (d) the Netherlands

* 8. What were some of the problems that Washington's soldiers faced at Valley Forge? (Select **all** that are correct.)

ⓐ sneak attacks by British soldiers

ⓑ lack of food

ⓒ poor shelter

ⓓ raids by local Indian tribes

ⓔ very cold weather and illness

9. Where was the last major battle of the Revolutionary War fought?

ⓐ Concord

ⓑ Yorktown

ⓒ Lexington

ⓓ Bunker Hill

10. What form of government did the new nation of the United States have?

ⓐ monarchy

ⓑ dictatorship

ⓒ mob rule

ⓓ republic

* 11. What happened as a result of Washington crossing the Delaware? (Select **two** that are correct.)

ⓐ Americans surprised the British and ended the Revolutionary War.

ⓑ Washington surprised the British and won the first important victory of the war.

ⓒ The French decided not to help the young United States.

ⓓ Americans started to believe they might win the war.

12. Why were colonists upset when the redcoats came to Boston?
   (a) The redcoats were not good at keeping order.
   (b) Colonists thought they were being treated like conquered people.
   (c) Colonists wanted redcoats to be sent to New York and Philadelphia, too.
   (d) The redcoats attacked the Boston Harbor.

13. What happened at Lexington and Concord?
   (a) The French decided to enter the war.
   (b) General Cornwallis surrendered to General Washington.
   (c) The first battles of the Revolutionary War were fought.
   (d) The Declaration of Independence was written and signed.

14. What was done to celebrate American independence?
   (a) The Liberty Bell was rung in Philadelphia.
   (b) Parliament opened the Port of Boston to merchant ships.
   (c) The minutemen marched around the Liberty Tree.
   (d) George Washington crossed the Delaware to spread the news.

15. Many American colonists trained themselves to be soldiers who could be ready to fight at short notice. What did they call themselves?
   (a) freedom fighters
   (b) Hessians
   (c) minutemen
   (d) redcoats

16. In what event before the Revolution did British soldiers fire on colonists?
    ⓐ Boston Massacre
    ⓑ Stamp Act
    ⓒ Boston Tea Party
    ⓓ Paul Revere's ride

* 17. Select all the true statements about Valley Forge. (Select **all** that are correct.)
    ⓐ Samuel Adams helped train the Continental Army there.
    ⓑ Many men suffered greatly while they camped there for the winter.
    ⓒ The Americans retreated there after the British captured Philadelphia.
    ⓓ A Spanish officer taught the army how to march correctly.
    ⓔ George Washington trained the army to be better.

18. What country's navy helped the Americans defeat the British at Yorktown?
    ⓐ Spain
    ⓑ England
    ⓒ Portugal
    ⓓ France

19. Which date is America's Independence Day?
    ⓐ November 11, 1607
    ⓑ July 1, 1776
    ⓒ July 4, 1776
    ⓓ October 19, 1781

20. Draw a line from each statement on the left to the famous person on the right who might have said it.

"I'm a colonist and a patriot. I formed a group called the Sons of Liberty to oppose the British Stamp Act."   George Washington

"I'm a colonist and a patriot. I rode my horse through the countryside warning the colonists that British troops were approaching."   Samuel Adams

"I was the leader who helped the soldiers through the rough winter at Valley Forge. I trained them to be a better army. There's a famous painting of me crossing the Delaware."   John Adams

"I worked very hard in Philadelphia to make sure all the colonies at the Second Continental Congress voted for the Declaration of Independence."   Paul Revere

21. Number the following events in the order in which they happened.

☐ The Battles of Lexington and Concord were fought.

☐ Cornwallis surrendered to Washington at Yorktown.

☐ Parliament passed the Stamp Act.

☐ The Declaration of Independence was signed.

22-24. Describe at least three obstacles faced by the American army during the Revolutionary War. Write in complete sentences.

_____

_____

_____

_____

_____

Student Guide
Lesson 10: Semester Review and Assessment

You've completed the second semester, and now it's time to review what you've learned and take the semester assessment.

Lesson Objectives

- Demonstrate mastery of important knowledge and skills in this semester.
- Demonstrate mastery of important knowledge and skills taught in previous lessons.
- State that the Ottoman Turks conquered Constantinople in 1453 and renamed it Istanbul.
- State that Hinduism was the main religion of India.
- Name the Mughal Empire as the powerful Muslim empire established in India.
- State that Akbar worked to make sure people of different religions could live together in peace.
- Describe the Taj Mahal as a beautiful tomb for Shah Jahan's wife.
- State that skilled craftsmen in Benin made beautiful works of art from brass.
- Explain that the Portuguese wanted slaves to work on sugar plantations in the New World.
- Explain some major effects of the transatlantic slave trade.
- List silk and porcelain as goods produced and traded by China.
- Explain that the Ming built the Great Wall to keep out invaders.
- Recognize that the Tokugawa were powerful rulers of Japan.
- Explain that early Tokugawa shoguns expelled Europeans from Japan.
- State that England became a powerful nation under Elizabeth's rule.
- State that Sir Francis Drake and the English navy defeated the Spanish Armada in 1588.
- Name William Shakespeare as the greatest English poet and playwright.
- Define "divine right of kings" as the belief that kings got their authority from God and not from the people.
- Explain that the Glorious Revolution was a bloodless revolution that made Parliament more powerful than the king.
- Explain that the first Americans crossed a land bridge to travel from Asia to North America.
- Name Jamestown as the first successful English settlement in North America.
- Describe Plymouth as a colony begun for religious freedom.
- Explain that Pennsylvania was founded for religious freedom for Quakers and others.
- State that Maryland was founded for religious freedom for Catholics.
- State that by the 1730s there were 13 English colonies on the east coast of North America.
- Define a plantation as a large farm that required a lot of laborers.
- Describe the colonists as proud to be English.
- State that American colonists objected to the Stamp Act.
- Identify July 4, 1776, as America's Independence Day.
- Describe some obstacles to American victory in the Revolutionary War.
- Describe Washington as the leader who got the soldiers through the winter and trained them to be a better army.
- Explain that the French blockade helped secure victory.

PREPARE

Approximate lesson time is 60 minutes.

Materials

For the Student

History Record Book

Keywords and Pronunciation

Akbar (AK-bur)

Benin (buh-NEEN)

English Parliament (PAHR-luh-muhnt) : The lawmaking body of England, including representatives of the nobility and of the commoners.

Mughal (MOO-guhl)

Niger (NIY-jur)

Ottoman (AH-tuh-muhn)

Shah Jahan (shah juh-HAHN)

Taj Mahal (tahj mah-HAHL)

Tokugawa (toh-kou-GAH-wuh)

LEARN

Activity 1: A Look Back (Offline)

Instructions

We've reached the year 1783 after taking a long trip through time. You've learned that while Renaissance artists and kings created great works in Christian Europe, amazing things were happening in the Muslim east as well. We studied two large Muslim empires. Can you remember their names? [1]

The Ottoman Empire began on the peninsula of Asia Minor. The Ottoman Turks grew so powerful they conquered the old Byzantine capital of Constantinople and gave it a new name. Do you remember the name? [2]

Istanbul became the capital of the Ottoman Empire. One of its most famous leaders, Süleyman, made sure Istanbul was a fabulous place. He built mosques, parks, and fountains. He also organized the laws for his empire, which was very large. It spread from Asia Minor through North Africa, into Arabia, and even into central Asia. Turkish merchants traded with others from all over the world.

Meanwhile, the Mughal Empire sprang up in India. In the 1500s, Muslim tribes rode east and conquered northern India. Eventually, the Mughals ruled most of the Indian subcontinent. That was tricky, because most of the people in India were not Muslim. Which religion did most of the people in India follow? [3]

One Muslim leader worked especially hard to figure out how people of all different religions could live together in peace. What was his name? [4]

Akbar's grandson, Shah Jahan, gave India its greatest building. Shah Jahan built it as a tomb for his wife. With its domes, reflecting pools, and marble writing, it became the greatest work of Muslim architecture in India. What is that building called? [5]

West of India and Arabia lay Africa. Much of north Africa had been conquered by the Ottomans. But along the Niger River, independent African kingdoms thrived. The kingdom of Benin was rich in pepper, ivory, and gold. The people of Benin built palaces and adorned their altars with beautiful brass work. The brass work of Benin was their pride and joy.

Benin grew richer as its people traded with the Portuguese. The rulers of Benin sold the Portuguese not only pepper and ivory, but also African slaves. A terrible slave trade began. What was that slave trade called? (Here's a hint: Think of the name of the ocean that slaves crossed to the New World.) [6]

Why did the Portuguese want slaves? [7]

Eventually, other Europeans would also buy slaves, including British planters in the North America. In a few years, so many African slaves were being sold to Europeans that the Europeans called the coast of Africa along the Niger River "the slave coast."

Renaissance Europeans traveled to China and Japan as well. There more amazing sights awaited them. In China, the Ming Dynasty had built a Forbidden City. Do you remember why it was called "forbidden"? [8]

The Ming also built a Great Wall. Why did they build that wall? [9]

Sometimes the Ming wished they could keep Europeans out of China, too. But European traders liked to buy Chinese silk and porcelain, so the Chinese traded with them when they could.

The Japanese also welcomed the Europeans with caution. At first the Japanese were happy to learn about Christianity and trade with the Europeans. Do you remember what the Portuguese sold the Japanese? [10]

Those guns helped the important Tokugawa family come to power. But when the Tokugawa emperors grew strong, they killed the Japanese who had become Christians and threw the Europeans out. They said, "Leave us alone!"

Meanwhile, life in Europe was very eventful. Henry VIII had made England Protestant. Now his lively, red-headed daughter came to the English throne. What was the name of this intelligent and important queen of England? [11]

Elizabeth ruled over England during its golden age. In the beginning of the golden age, the king of Spain thought he should conquer England. He sent the Spanish Armada to do the job. Do you remember what happened? Surprise! The English won the battle at sea. Men like Sir Francis Drake and Sir Walter Raleigh defeated the Spanish Armada. Elizabeth set about building the English navy and making England great. William Shakespeare helped make England great, too. He wrote while Elizabeth was queen. Who was Shakespeare? [12]

Queen and commoner came to watch Shakespeare's plays at the Globe. And England became great in other ways. It started to establish colonies in North America.

After Elizabeth died, the British Parliament and the Stuart kings competed for power. Finally Parliament did something very important. In 1688, Parliament threw out one king and invited in another. That bloodless revolution was called the Glorious Revolution. It told every monarch afterward that in England, kings ruled with the consent of Parliament. Parliament, not the king, would make England's laws. England had a proud heritage of liberty.

Nobody was prouder of that English heritage of liberty than English colonists in North America. Those colonists were a feisty bunch. Some came to America to get rich. Many came for religious freedom. Can you remember the names of some of the groups who came to America for religious freedom? [13] Many colonists, like the English debtors in Georgia, came for freedom to start a new life. Some wanted cheap land and a chance to farm.

After Jamestown, the king knew England wasn't going to get rich from its colonies. So the king and Parliament usually let the colonists alone. If people weren't happy with their life in England, chances were they could find a home in one of the colonies. Before long, there were thirteen rowdy British colonies lining the Atlantic coast.

They all got rowdier in 1776. Why is that year important? [14]

Sam Adams, John Adams, Thomas Jefferson, George Washington, the Sons of Liberty, and the minutemen all helped make American independence happen. What was the name of the long war that followed? [15]

The American Revolution started out as a war for English rights and liberties. It ended up as the start of a brand new country--the United States of America, the first republic of modern times.

Whew! What a journey. And next year, the story goes on. Democracy spreads. Slavery ends. Wars start. New nations are born. People live longer and communicate faster than ever before. Will they understand each other better? That's a question for next year.

Activity 2: End of Semester! *(Online)*

ASSESS

Semester Assessment: History 3, Semester 2 *(Offline)*

Complete an offline Semester Assessment. Your learning coach will score this part of the assessment.

Name _____   Date _____

Semester Assessment

Read each question and its answer choices. Fill in the bubble in front of the word or words that best answer the question.

Questions marked with an asterisk (*) will have more than one correct answer. For these questions, fill in the bubble next to ALL correct answers.

1. When the Ottoman Empire conquered the city of Constantinople, they changed the city's name to
   ⓐ Benin
   ⓑ Istanbul
   ⓒ Alexandria
   ⓓ Mohenjo Daro

2. What is the name of the building Shah Jahan built in India as a tomb for his wife?
   ⓐ Grand Bazaar
   ⓑ Hagia Sophia
   ⓒ Taj Mahal
   ⓓ Süleymaniye

3. What was the name of the powerful Muslim empire founded by Babur in India?
   ⓐ Mughal Empire
   ⓑ Ottoman Empire
   ⓒ Empire of the Akbars
   ⓓ Kingdom of Benin

4. What Muslim leader worked hard to find ways that people of different religions could live together in peace?

    ⓐ Ieyasu

    ⓑ Akbar

    ⓒ Süleyman

    ⓓ Shah Jahan

5. Which religion did most of the people of India follow?

    ⓐ Christianity

    ⓑ Islam

    ⓒ Judaism

    ⓓ Hinduism

6. What was the African kingdom of Benin known for?

    ⓐ the porcelain vases they made for foreigners

    ⓑ the brass sculptures they made for their altars

    ⓒ the silk cloth they wove for their kings and queens

    ⓓ the sugarcane they grew to be sent to Portugal

7. How did the transatlantic slave trade begin?

    ⓐ England started buying slaves to serve settlers in Jamestown.

    ⓑ Spain started buying slaves to help them fight the Aztecs.

    ⓒ Portugal started buying slaves to farm sugar plantations in Brazil.

    ⓓ China started buying slaves to work on silk farms.

8. What did European merchants buy from the Chinese?

    ⓐ silk and porcelain

    ⓑ pepper and cotton

    ⓒ brass sculptures and gold

    ⓓ muskets and mirrors

9. Why did the Ming dynasty build the Great Wall?
- (a) to keep merchants from leaving
- (b) to divide the country into two kingdoms
- (c) to keep invading Mongols out
- (d) to protect travelers along the Spice Road

10. What family came to power in Japan with the help of muskets shortly after the Portuguese arrived?
- (a) Mongol
- (b) Tokugawa
- (c) Ming
- (d) Mughal

11. What happened when the Japanese rulers began to fear and distrust the Europeans?
- (a) They started trading silk for ivory with African kingdoms.
- (b) They sent a fleet of ships to attack Italian ports.
- (c) They built walls along their coasts to keep people out.
- (d) They made Europeans leave Japan and then turned inward.

12. England became a powerful nation and experienced a golden age while I was queen. Who am I?
- (a) Eleanor
- (b) Elizabeth
- (c) Isabella
- (d) Mary

13. What happened in 1588 that made England a major sea power?
  (a) Spain tried to invade England, but its armada was defeated.
  (b) Portugal tried to invade England, but its armada was defeated.
  (c) The English navy destroyed France's merchant fleet.
  (d) English explorers founded permanent colonies in North America.

14. Who was England's most famous playwright and poet?
  (a) Walter Raleigh
  (b) Francis Drake
  (c) John Smith
  (d) William Shakespeare

15. What country was England's major enemy during the Elizabethan era?
  (a) Japan
  (b) Germany
  (c) Spain
  (d) Portugal

16. During the reign of Elizabeth I, what did England begin to do?
  (a) explore and colonize South America
  (b) explore and colonize North America
  (c) send merchants to African kingdoms
  (d) fight and defeat the Aztecs and Incas

17. King James believed in the divine right of kings. What was that?
  (a) The belief that kings should be worshipped as gods.
  (b) The belief that kings should protect the rights of the people.
  (c) The belief that kings got their authority from God and didn't have to answer to the people.
  (d) The belief that kings should have rights no god could take away.

18. After the Glorious Revolution, who made the laws in England?
ⓐ the Parliament
ⓑ the king
ⓒ the Puritans
ⓓ the pope

19. During the 1600s and 1700s, where did most European settlers to North America come from?
ⓐ France
ⓑ England
ⓒ Spain
ⓓ Portugal

20. What was the first permanent English settlement in North America?
ⓐ Jamestown
ⓑ Plymouth
ⓒ Philadelphia
ⓓ New York

21. How did the settling of the southern colonies in America affect the transatlantic slave trade?
ⓐ Fewer slaves were brought over because there were enough colonists to work the plantations.
ⓑ More slaves were brought over because the northern colonies needed them.
ⓒ More slaves were brought over because plantations required a lot of workers.
ⓓ The settling of the southern colonies had no effect on the transatlantic slave trade.

22. The first people to settle the American continents _____.
  ⓐ sailed over from Africa
  ⓑ sailed over from Europe
  ⓒ walked over a land bridge from Asia
  ⓓ walked over a land bridge from South America

23. Many colonists came to America for religious freedom. Which of the following were started for religious freedom?
  ⓐ Pennsylvania, Georgia, and Plymouth
  ⓑ Plymouth, Maryland, and Georgia
  ⓒ Jamestown, Maryland, and Pennsylvania
  ⓓ Maryland, Massachusetts Bay, and Pennsylvania

24. By 1750, how many British colonies were there along the east coast of North America?
  ⓐ 3
  ⓑ 7
  ⓒ 13
  ⓓ 50

25. In what year did the American colonists declare their independence from Great Britain?
  ⓐ 1607
  ⓑ 1688
  ⓒ 1776
  ⓓ 1783

26. Which of the following best describes the colonists *before 1760*?
   (a) They were proud to be English and were happy with England.
   (b) They were embarrassed to be English and were unhappy with England.
   (c) They thought of themselves as Americans and wanted their independence.
   (d) They hated England because they felt they had few rights and liberties.

27. What act of Parliament angered the colonists and started them on the path to revolution?
   (a) the Boston Massacre
   (b) the Battle of Lexington
   (c) the Stamp Act
   (d) the Act of Liberty

28. I'm the commander in chief of the Continental Army. I crossed the Delaware River to surprise our enemies and trained my men at Valley Forge. Who am I?
   (a) Thomas Jefferson
   (b) George Washington
   (c) Samuel Adams
   (d) Paul Revere

29. What country fought on the side of the colonies and helped them win the war against Great Britain?
   (a) Portugal
   (b) Spain
   (c) France
   (d) the Netherlands

* 30. What were some of the obstacles the Americans faced during the Revolutionary War? (Select **all** that are correct.)

   ⓐ England had the most powerful navy in the world.

   ⓑ Spanish soldiers were fighting alongside British troops.

   ⓒ The American army did not have enough weapons and supplies.

   ⓓ The British army used minutemen as soldiers to fight on short notice.

Answer Keys

Lesson Assessment Answer Key

The Rising Ottoman Turks

Answers:

1. The Asian Minor is below the Black Sea.
2. The Black Sea is above the Asian Minor.
3. the Ottoman Turks
4. Constantinople
5. Istanbul

Lesson Assessment Answer Key

Süleyman, the Lawgiver

Answers:

1. Use the map key to locate the Ottoman Empire.
2. Süleyman
3. larger
4. He organized the Islamic laws of the Ottoman Empire so that everyone followed the same laws.

Lesson Assessment Answer Key

The Trading Turks

Answers:

1. trade
2. possible answers: silk, perfume, soap, spices, gold, wool, fur, rugs
3. possible answers: North Africa, Europe, Arabia, India, China
4. crescent and star

Lesson Assessment Answer Key

Mughals Victorious in India

Answers:

1. The Indian Subcontinent comprises the majority of the map.
2. the Indus and the Ganges
3. for its treasures such as spices and gems
4. Hinduism
5. the Mughal Empire

Lesson Assessment Answer Key

Akbar the Wise

Answers:

1. the Mughal Empire
2. Islam
3. No, Akbar was interested in all religions.
4. Akbar worked to make sure they could all live together in peace.

Lesson Assessment Answer Key

Shah Jahan Builds the Taj Mahal

Answers:

1. Shah Jahan

2. to have a beautiful tomb for his wife

3. possible answers: very tall domes, slender towers or minarets, beautiful marble, gardens

4.

Looking East: Ottomans and Mughals: Answer Key

1. Ottoman Turks

2. Istanbul

3. crescent and star

4. Hinduism

5. Taj Mahal

6. Süleyman

7. trade

8. Asia Minor

9. Istanbul

10.

11. large, expanding Muslim empires

12. Akbar

13. Hinduism and Islam

14.

15. the Ottoman Empire

Lesson Assessment Answer Key

Benin Grows

Answers:

1. The kingdom of Benin is on the western side of Africa.
2. brass
3. from trade

Lesson Assessment Answer Key

The New Slave Trade: East and West

Answers:

1. to farm the sugar plantations in Brazil
2. across the Atlantic Ocean
3. Many died; many were taken to the New World to work on plantations.
4. They grew rich from trading slaves.

Name _____   Date _____

Lesson Assessment Answer Key

The Ming Dynasty and a Forbidden City

Answers:

1. an important Chinese dynasty

2. Beijing

3. the home of the Ming emperor

4. Possible answers: red brick walls; yellow tile roofs; sculpted stone staircases; dragons or animal guardians on roofs; many gates, rooms and halls.

Lesson Assessment Answer Key

Chinese Trade in the Age of Exploration

Answers:

1. a Chinese explorer
2. They were suspicious of Europeans; they wanted to keep them in just one place.
3. Spain and Portugal
4. silk and porcelain

Lesson Assessment Answer Key

Rebuilding the Great Wall

Answers:

1. to keep out Mongol invaders.

2. the Great Wall of China

3. Possible answers: It was made of stone and brick; it had signal towers; six horses could ride on it side-by-side; it was built by many, many workers; it stretched for thousands of miles.

Lesson Assessment Answer Key

The Portuguese in Feudal Japan

Answers:

1. A kingdom of many islands
2. a feudal system
3. at war
4. to trade and to spread Christianity

Name _____ Date _____

Lesson Assessment Answer Key

The Tokugawa Shoguns Throw the Foreigners Out

Answers:

1. the main military ruler of Japan
2. a family that ruled as shoguns for a long time
3. They made foreigners leave Japan.

Name _____ Date _____

Lesson Assessment Answer Key

Africa, China, and Japan

Answers:

1. brass
2. to work on sugar plantations
3. Beijing
4. silk
   porcelain
5. to keep invading armies out
6. feudal
7. Tokugawa
8. Benin grew and became wealthier.
9. The Portuguese began exploring and farming in South America.
10. Any two of the following:
    red brick walls
    yellow tile roofs
    sculpted stone staircases
    dragons or animals on the roof
11. Spain
    Portugal
12. Daimyos and samurai were fighting to gain power.
13. They made Europeans leave Japan and persecuted Christians.

14.

Benin	China	Japan
brass art	Great Wall	Edo
slave trade	silk and porcelain	Tokugawa shogunate
spices and ivory	Ming dynasty	feudal system
	Beijing	
	Forbidden city	

15. Characteristics of the Great Wall of China include the following: It was made of stone and brick; it had signal towers; six horses could fit side by side on the top; it was built by many workers; it stretched for thousands of miles

16. False

17.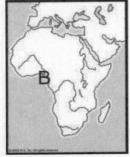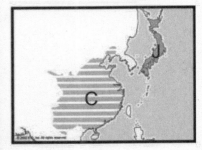

Lesson Assessment Answer Key

Elizabeth I: Her Father's Daughter

Answers:

1. Elizabeth I
2. possible answers include: religious divisions, possible war with Spain, the people not accustomed to being ruled by a woman
3. a golden age
4. the Elizabethan era
5. more powerful

Lesson Assessment Answer Key

Sir Francis Drake

Answers:

1. Spain and Portugal
2. a daring English sea captain or "sea dog"
3. He attacked Spanish and Portuguese treasure ships.
4. around the world

Name _____ Date _____

Lesson Assessment Answer Key

Defeat of the Spanish Armada

Answers:

1. a fleet of armed Spanish ships that tried to attack England
2. Sir Francis Drake
3. No, it failed.
4. England became a great sea power.

Name _____   Date _____

Lesson Assessment Answer Key

Go Forth, Sir Walter!

Answers:

1. Sir Walter Raleigh

2. He wanted to explore and go on sea expeditions.

3. Roanoke, Roanoke Island

Lesson Assessment Answer Key

Shakespeare: England's Bard

Answers:

1. William Shakespeare

2. plays

3. the Elizabethan Era

4. any two of the following: majestic, hint, hurry, bump, lovely, excellent, gloomy, vanished into thin air, refused to budge an inch, tongue-tied, hoodwinked, in a pickle, too much of a good thing, sleep a wink, leapfrog, football, jig, mountaineer, shooting star, hush, wild-goose chase, lonely, quarrelsome, fretful

Lesson Assessment Answer Key

Stewing the Stuarts

Answers:

1. the Stuarts
2. King James I
3. the belief that kings got their authority from God and not from the people
4. Parliament

Lesson Assessment Answer Key

A Glorious Revolution

Answers:

1. It was short-lived.
2. William and Mary
3. It was bloodless.
4. Parliament
5. He promised to keep the laws made by Parliament.

Unit Assessment Answer Key

England's Golden Age and Beyond: Answer Key

Answers:

1. Elizabeth I
2. an English sea captain who made a voyage around the world
3. The English navy defeated the Spanish Armada.
4. Walter Raleigh
5. an English playwright and poet
6. God
7. Elizabeth I
8. Spain
9. Elizabeth I
10. explore and colonize North America
11. a fleet of armed Spanish ships defeated by the English
12. He was an explorer.
    He was a favorite of Elizabeth I.
    He attempted to start a colony on Roanoke.
13. Parliament
14. the Glorious Revolution
15. the Stuarts

Name _____   Date _____

Lesson Assessment Answer Key

The First Americans

Answers:

1. by crossing a land bridge from Asia
2. whales and seals
3. desert
4. possible answers: corn, beans, squash

Lesson Assessment Answer Key

People of the Plains and Forest

Answers:

1. The Rocky Mountains are on the western side of the United States. The Appalachian Mountains are on the eastern side. The Great Plains is the area between the two mountain ranges. The Mississippi River runs from just west of the Great Lakes to the Gulf of Mexico.

2. They ate buffalo and used its hide for clothing, shelter, and even boats.

3. forests, woods

4. Mandan

5. Iroquois, Mohawk, Seneca, Cayuga, Onondaga, Oneida or Creek

Lesson Assessment Answer Key

The Story of Jamestown

Answers:

1. Jamestown
2. gold
3. John Smith
4. possible answers: lazy gentleman settlers, disease, starvation, Indian attacks

Name _____ Date _____

Lesson Assessment Answer Key
The Story of Plymouth Colony

Answers:

1. Possible answers: They were persecuted in England; they wanted to live in a place where they could worship as they pleased.

2. the *Mayflower*

3. possible answers: the Indians; Squanto

4. They taught the the Pilgrims to plant corn, which berries to eat and how to catch eels.

5. a festival to thank God for the harvest

Lesson Assessment Answer Key

The Story of William Penn

Answers:

1. Puritans

2. William Penn

3. so Quakers and others could have religious freedom; so people of all religions could live together in peace

4. City of Brotherly Love

Lesson Assessment Answer Key

More Colonists in Maryland and Georgia

Answers:

1. Maryland
2. debtors
3. 13

Name

Date

Mapping the Thirteen Colonies

Follow the directions in the box below. On the next page, fill in the blanks to show information about four of the colonies.

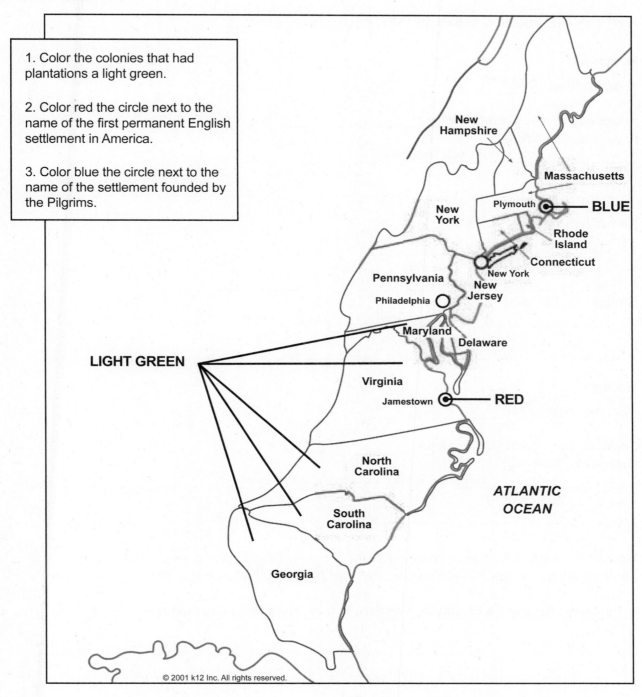

1. Color the colonies that had plantations a light green.

2. Color red the circle next to the name of the first permanent English settlement in America.

3. Color blue the circle next to the name of the settlement founded by the Pilgrims.

Name _____ Date _____

Mapping the Thirteen Colonies

Fill in the blanks to show information about four of the colonies.

New York was originally settled by the **Dutch** _____.

Maryland

Year founded: **1634** _____

Founded by **the Calvert family** _____
Reason for founding:
_____ **religious freedom** _____

_____

Pennsylvania

Year founded: **1682** _____

Founded by **William Penn** _____
Reason for founding:
_____ **religious freedom** _____

_____

Georgia

Year founded: **1733** _____

Founded by **James Oglethorpe** _____
Reason for founding:
_____ **to give debtors a chance to start over** _____

_____

Most of the early colonists were from England, but some colonists came from other countries. Name three countries that some of the colonists came from.

Germany, Ireland, Netherlands, Sweden, France, Finland, Spain, Portugal

_____

Lesson Assessment Answer Key

From Many Lands

Answers:

1. the Dutch

2. possible answers: Native Americans, Dutch, Finns, Swedes, Germans, Scotch-Irish, Portuguese and Spanish Jews, Africans

3. a plantation

4. by using slavery

Unit Assessment Answer Key

The America They Found and Founded

Answers:

1. They walked over a land bridge from Asia.

2. Pacific Northwest: hunted whales and seals; built large seagoing canoes
   Southwestern (Pueblo): lived in the desert; grew corn
   Plains: hunted buffalo for food and clothing
   Eastern Woodland: lived in the forests; hunted and farmed; grew corn, beans, and squash

3. to find gold

4. John Smith

5. New York: the Dutch; E.
   Plymouth: Pilgrims; D.
   Pennsylvania: William Penn; C.
   Maryland: Lord George Calvert; B.
   Georgia: James Oglethorpe; A.

6. Plantations required a lot of workers.

7. 13; North America

8. people with unusual ideas who wanted a new start

9.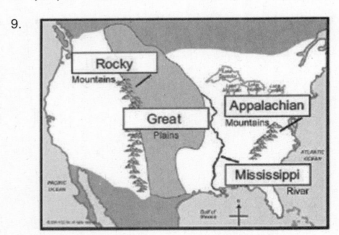

10. England

11. Jamestown

12. Puritans

13. help from the Indians

14. The colonies all had English laws and an English way of life.

15. _3_ Georgia is founded as a colony for debtors.
    _1_ The first Americans cross a land bridge into North America.
    _2_ The English settle in Jamestown.

16. Plantations existed in the southern colonies.
Plantations required a lot of workers.
Plantation owners began using African slaves.

17. **Writing sample:** The settlers' experience at Jamestown was very hard. The land was swampy and full of mosquitoes. It was also in the territory of the Powhatan Indians. Many of the settlers were used to having servants to do their work. They weren't used to doing hard work themselves. They were busy looking for gold instead of learning to survive. Many of the settlers drank bad water from the river and the swamps and became sick. Settlers began to die. The Indians grew tired of the settlers and stopped helping them. They even attacked Jamestown. During the cold winter the settlers ate all of the stored food and all of the animals. People stayed inside the settlement because they were afraid of the Indians. The colonists began starving to death.

Scoring: This question is worth forty points. Award ten points for each of the following facts that the student addresses correctly in writing, up to a maximum of forty points:

- Jamestown was swampy and mosquito infested.

- Jamestown was located in the territory of the Powhatan Indians, who were not happy about the strangers being there and even attacked the settlers.

- Disease broke out because of bad water from the river and the swamps.

- There was not enough food; colonists were starving to death.

- It was a very cold winter.

- The settlers were busy looking for gold when they arrived.

- Many settlers were used to having servants do their work; they weren't used to doing hard work themselves.

Reading Graphs Answer Key

Activity 12: Graphs

1. 7 maple trees
2. 12 spruce trees
3. 10 oak trees
4. spruce, oak, maple, willow
5. 8 cm
6. 6 cm
7. October
8. July
9. Gray stands for stone houses. Tan stands for wood houses.
10. Seven houses are made of brick.
11. Ten houses are made of stone.
12. Three houses are made of wood.
13. Wood was used least often.
14. Stone was used most often.
15. There are 20 houses.
16. Yes; yes

Skill Builder
1. picture graph, bar graph, circle graph
2. pie chart
3. stone
4. Answers may vary. Bar graphs could show many different things, including rainfall and temperature.
5. Answers may vary. You could show anything that can be divided into its parts.

Reading a Time Line Answer Key

Activity 13: Time Lines

1. Spanish soldiers establish a fort at St. Augustine in Florida in 1565.
2. The Declaration of Independence is signed in Philadelphia, Pennsylvania, in 1776.
3. British colonists settle at Jamestown, Virginia, in 1607 and the pilgrims arrive at Plymouth, Massachusetts, in 1620.
4. The Pilgrims arrived in 1620.
5. The British settled Jamestown in 1607.
6. The finger should be placed just to the left of the 1733 entry.
7. The time line shows 250 years.
8. Accept either 10 or 11 years—but point out that if you include both 1775 and 1785 there are 11 years.
9. 1781
10. 1775
11. winter at Valley Forge
12. **Optional:** the signing of the Declaration of Independence
13. **Optional:** American soldiers spend the winter at Valley Forge.
14. **Optional:** George Washington leads the Continental Army.
15. Georgia
16. Virginia
17. Philadelphia
18. Pennsylvania
19. Plymouth, Massachusetts
20. St. Augustine, Florida

Skill Builder
1. Time lines can help you remember the order in which important events took place.
2. Answers may vary, but could include the years the members of a family were born or any series of events.

Lesson Assessment Answer Key

Reading a Time Line

Answers:

1. Declaration of Independence
2. American soldiers spent the winter at Valley Forge
3. 1783
4. 1565
5. 1733

Lesson Assessment Answer Key

English and Proud of It!

Answers:

1. The colonists were proud of having rights and enjoying liberty, or freedom.

2. The colonists had their own assemblies that they elected.

3. They were proud to be English.

Name _____ Date _____

Lesson Assessment Answer Key

No Taxation Without Representation!

Answers:

1. They hated it.
2. It meant the colonists should not be taxed by Parliament, where they had no representatives.
3. He was an American patriot.
4. Possible answers: He started the Sons of Liberty; he led people against the Stamp Act.
5. a group started by Samuel Adams to fight the British tax

Name _____   Date _____

Lesson Assessment Answer Key

The First Clashes

Answers:

1. Possible answers: They were angry about the soldiers being there; they resented them; they thought the king was trying to take away their freedom.

2. American farmers who trained as soldiers to be able to fight in a minute

3. the Boston Massacre

4. They threw tea on ships overboard into the harbor.

5. the Boston Tea Party

Lesson Assessment Answer Key

Lexington, Concord, and Bunker Hill

Answers:

1. Paul Revere
2. They were the first battles of the Revolutionary War.
3. the minutemen
4. They showed them that the Americans were ready and willing to fight.

Name _____ Date _____

Lesson Assessment Answer Key

The Declaration of Independence

Answers:

1. the document that said the American colonies were free from England and had formed their own country

2. the United States of America

3. July 4, 1776

4. the bell that was rung to celebrate American independence

5.

Lesson Assessment Answer Key

Crossing the Delaware and Getting Help from the French

Answers:

1. Possible answers: They were fighting the powerful British army and navy; they did not have much equipment or training; they lost some early battles and some territory.

2. Washington crossing the Delaware on Christmas night

3. It gave Americans hope for a chance of victory over the British.

4. France

Lesson Assessment Answer Key

Winter at Valley Forge

Answers:

1. a time of hardship and suffering
2. cold; not enough food, clothing or shelter
3. George Washington

Lesson Assessment Answer Key

Victory at Yorktown

Answers:

1. Yorktown
2. Cornwallis
3. France
4. a Republic

Unit Assessment Answer Key

The American Revolution

Answers:

1. They were proud of their rights and liberties and proud to be English.

2. colonial assemblies

3. No taxation without representation!

4. They were being taxed without their consent.

5. Colonists dumped tea into Boston Harbor to protest the tax on it.

6. Declaration of Independence

7. France

8. lack of food
   poor shelter
   very cold weather and illness

9. Yorktown

10. republic

11. Washington surprised the British and won the first important victory of the war.
    Americans started to believe they might win the war.

12. Colonists thought they were being treated like conquered people.

13. The first battles of the Revolutionary War were fought.

14. The Liberty Bell was rung in Philadelphia.

15. minutemen

16. Boston Massacre

17. Many men suffered greatly while they camped there for the winter.
    The Americans retreated there after the British captured Philadelphia.
    George Washington trained the army to be better.

18. France

19. July 4, 1776

20. "I'm a colonist and a patriot. I formed a group called the Sons of Liberty to oppose the British Stamp Act." **-Samuel Adams**

    "I'm a colonist and a patriot. I rode my horse through the countryside warning the colonists that British troops were approaching." **-Paul Revere**

    "I was the leader who helped the soldiers through the rough winter at Valley Forge. I trained them to be a better army. There's a famous painting of me crossing the Delaware." **-George Washington**

    "I worked very hard in Philadelphia to make sure all the colonies at the Second Continental Congress voted for the Declaration of Independence." **-John Adams**

21. _2_ The Battles of Lexington and Concord were fought.

   _4_ Cornwallis surrendered to Washington at Yorktown.

   _1_ Parliament passed the Stamp Act.

   _3_ The Declaration of Independence was signed.

22. Writing sample: The American army faced many obstaclesduring the Revolutionary War. The British navy was the most powerful in the world. The British also had a large, strong army. The American army wasn't made up of real soldiers. They were farmers fighting. They were not very well trained. The American army didn't have enough weapons and uniforms. These are some of the things that made it hard for the colonies to win the war.

Scoring: This question is worth thirty points. Award ten point for each fact that the student addresses correctly, up to a maximum of thirty points. The following are possible facts that could be included:

-England had the best (largest, most powerful) navy in the world.
-England's army was one of the best in the world.
-The American army wasn't made up of professional soldiers, just farmers.
-The American army (Continental Army) was poorly trained.
-The American army didn't have enough weapons and uniforms.
-Congress was slow about sending them money for supplies.

Name _____   Date _____

Semester Assessment Answer Key

History 3, Semester 2

Answers:

1. Istanbul
2. Taj Mahal
3. Mughal Empire
4. Akbar
5. Hinduism
6. the brass sculptures they made for their altars
7. Portugal started buying slaves to farm sugar plantations in Brazil.
8. silk and porcelain
9. to keep invading Mongols out
10. Tokugawa
11. They made Europeans leave Japan and then turned inward.
12. Elizabeth
13. Spain tried to invade England, but its armada was defeated.
14. William Shakespeare
15. Spain
16. explore and colonize North America
17. The belief that kings got their authority from God and didn't have to answer to the people.
18. the Parliament
19. England
20. Jamestown
21. More slaves were brought over because plantations required a lot of workers.
22. walked over a land bridge from Asia
23. Maryland, Massachusetts Bay, and Pennsylvania
24. 13
25. 1776
26. They were proud to be English and were happy with England.
27. the Stamp Act
28. George Washington
29. France
30. England had the most powerful navy in the world.
    The American army did not have enough weapons and supplies.